CUCINA FRESCA

VIANA LA PLACE

cucina fresca

EVAN KLEIMAN

illustrations by ann field

1817

HARPER & ROW, PUBLISHERS
New York, Cambridge, Philadelphia, San Francisco, London, Mexico City, São Paulo, Singapore, Sydney

Library of Congress Cataloging in Publication Data
LaPlace, Viana.
  Cucina fresca.
  Includes index.
  1. Cookery, Italian. 2. Cookery (Cold dishes)
I. Kleiman, Evan. II. Title.
TX830.L37 1985   641.5'55   84-48466
ISBN 0-06-181489-X
        85 86 87 88 89 MPV 10 9 8 7 6 5 4 3 2 1
ISBN 0-06-096000-0 (pbk.)
        85 86 87 88 89 MPV 10 9 8 7 6 5 4 3 2 1

TO
OUR PARENTS, EDITH KLEIMAN
ANTONIETTA AND PIERRE LA PLACE
WHO TAUGHT US HOW TO TASTE

Cuisine is when things taste like themselves.

—Curnosky

I am of the opinion that most food tastes better cold anyway. A chicken roasted and allowed to cool slowly is a far more delicious dish to me than a chicken hot from the oven. Likewise, steak perfectly broiled, seasoned, cooled and sliced thin is even more succulent than steak rushed from the grill. Vegetables, too, seem to have more flavor when cold, and they lend themselves to a great variety of dressings and sauces.

—James Beard

CONTENTS

ACKNOWLEDGMENTS

Writing a book can be a long and arduous process. Our load was lightened considerably and our time made more enjoyable because of the help and encouragement of those around us.

Teresa Joseph was the first person to see our fledgling writings. She helped us shape the manuscript into a professional effort and along the way a friendship grew. We are deeply appreciative.

Thanks to our friends and families who ate what we tested, commented, dealt with anxieties, and in general gave us support while we wrote this book. Heartfelt thanks to Jim Krupka and Michele Saie for their loving support. Loving thanks to Maria and Michelle La Place, Caterina Cammarata, Ester Lawrence, Ivan Thillet, Lydia and Maria Sarno, and John and Carla Strobel. Thanks to Carla and Susan for typing under pressure.

A special thank you to Maureen and Eric Lasher for giving us this opportunity and to our editor, Ann Bramson, for her warm encouragement and generous spirit.

CUCINA FRESCA

INTRODUCTION

Every collaboration has a beginning. This is how ours started:

We met in 1981 while cooking at Mangia, a simple trattoria which was the first Tuscan restaurant in Los Angeles. We found in each other an ally, an enthusiastic educated audience for the foods we both love to eat and cook. Our excitement in finding kindred spirits spurred exploration, as did the wealth of top-quality produce, oils, and imported cheeses available to us.

We talked food and cooked food daily, and our book grew out of those conversations and experiments which we continued when we both moved to the restaurant Verdi in Santa Monica.

As we got to know one another we discovered all that we shared in common. We were both born in Los Angeles in the early 1950s and raised there. We both experienced Los Angeles as a quiet, slow place of backyards, palm trees, and neighbors' swimming pools—a perfect place for dreaming. In a period when frozen and processed foods found their way onto practically every table, our families served simple fresh foods. This easy, open relationship with food encouraged in us adventurous tastes not found in many children. And so our tastes began to form and grow.

New experiences widened our worlds. We each took our first trip to Europe at an early age: Viana at twelve, Evan at sixteen. In due course we entered college. Evan attended UCLA where she studied Italian literature and film. Viana studied art at UC Berkeley, and while there was influenced by Berkeley's burgeoning food scene. During this period we again traveled to Europe although we went at different times and under different circumstances—Viana on family trips that resulted in a heightened awareness of her Italian heritage and Evan to study Italy's language and culture. A new world was revealed to us and at its center was food.

We both fell in love with the antipasti, their variety, beauty, and ease of preparation. We were amazed at the voluptuous beauty of European fruit and vegetable stands. The food spoke to our senses in pristine, white-tiled cheese shops where fresh cheeses floated in water, mascarpone came wrapped in pastel tissue, and creamy cheeses were bathed in oil; in markets where crunchy red and yellow peppers picked at their peak of flavor were bursting with sweetness. In dark shops bottles of olive oil were displayed, from the palest straw yellow to the deepest green. Just strolling through the central market in Florence was like going to a festival. Bouquets of flowers and branches blossoming with fresh hot red peppers stood in vases of water, and herbs of all types were tucked into corners of displays everywhere. Breads of all sizes and shapes, from tiny little rolls like rosettes to huge coarse loaves, were waiting to be cut into chunks and dipped into fruity olive oil. Tiny fragile heads and leaves of lettuces of staggering variety were lovingly displayed, giving the overall impression of a meadow. An incredible range of creatures from the sea in shades of white, pale pink, and iridescent black made us realize the variety of tastes yet to be sampled. At those moments we really understood the connection between nature and the art of nourishing ourselves actually and spiritually.

What we experienced in Italy had a profound effect on each of us. It was too exciting to leave behind. In spite of our studies in other fields and other commitments, we kept returning to cooking and sharing food until it finally became the central focus in our lives.

Cucina Fresca captures the spirit of the food we love. Two simple words express our point of view: *cucina* translates as kitchen, cuisine, cooking, and the food itself; *fresca* means fresh, new, and cool in temperature.

In *Cucina Fresca* the tastes of the Italian kitchen are treated in a light modern manner. There is the aromatic perfume of basil, rosemary, and sage; the rich flavor of garlic; the piquancy of *agrodolce* (sweet and sour), as well as the techniques basic to Italian cooking— especially the extensive use of grilling and marination. All the foods in this book are served at temperatures ranging from barely warm to cool but most fall happily into the category of room temperature. We know from our experience that the true flavors of food can be best appreciated at these temperatures. Much of our food can be prepared in advance, from a roasted chicken served just as it cools to roasted peppers marinated in oil for several days. These recipes are not prepared at the expense of a cook too weary and too nervous to sit with the guests. Our cooking is relaxed, fun, and removed from the pressures of last-minute execution. There is time to appreciate the raw ingredients, smell a ripe red tomato, or marvel at the papery mauve peel of the garlic.

Italian cuisine is often classed as a heavy cuisine with long-simmering sauces and enormous portions. We couldn't disagree more. In fact, we think there's a strong link between Italy's Cucina Fresca and the new California cuisine, the same emphasis on the freshest possible regional products, on fresh rather than dried herbs, the same use of grilling and marination, and the abundant use of vegetables. In *Cucina Fresca* we share with you light, fresh, and colorful foods that satisfy the way we want to eat today. Beautiful food, simply prepared and shared with friends and family, is one of the most basic and satisfying pleasures of life. All that's needed is a warm heart, a keen eye for the best ingredients, and a willing sense of adventure to lead you to a good place at the table.

BASICS

In *Cucina Fresca* we espouse an attitude that is removed from culinary one-upmanship and complex techniques, one in which the preparation of food is unbelabored, the finished product flavorful and visually vivid. Although our attitude is relaxed, our feelings about certain basic ingredients and techniques are well defined.

ANCHOVIES

"Hold the anchovies" is a phrase you will never hear us utter. It's a shame they have the reputation they do. What people might assume to be a strong fishy presence instead translates into added depth of flavor. When using anchovies, use salt sparingly. Purchase flat fillets packed in olive oil.

BREAD

Breadmaking is our link with the past. With three simple ingredients—flour, water, and leavening—the food that is a primary staple in the Western world is created. Bread is a touchstone for the degree to which a country has maintained its integrity in cooking. It seems that we in America have lost that primary connection to the "staff of life," seeing our over-refined, presliced bread as a vehicle for butter or as the afterthought that sandwich filling goes between.

What is a good loaf of bread? The bread we prefer is generally heavier than the standard American loaf. It is not sweet. The texture of the crumb is dense, sometimes chewy, coarse-grained and moist; the crust is crunchy and chewy, yet yielding. It is almost always better at room temperature than hot from the oven. This rustic loaf does not merely complement the meal, it can ·be an intrinsic element—in its own way as important as the meat course or dessert. A thick slice of bread, lightly toasted, drizzled with fragrant olive oil and slathered with Ricotta with Herbs (see page 93), or rubbed with the cut side of a ripe tomato, accompanied by a hearty glass of red wine and some briny black olives, can make a meal.

Grissini—Italian breadsticks—are also wonderful with foods. We can make a meal of grissini and prosciutto. These crisp, crunchy accompaniments range in texture from thin and delicate to coarse and crusty. Sizes range from three inches to over a foot long. You can purchase them plain or with sesame or poppy seeds. The best sources of good grissini are high-quality Italian bakeries or Italian specialty shops.

Of all foods, bread transcends the simple act of eating. When bread is broken, it nourishes body and soul.

BRUSCHETTE AND CROSTINI

Waverley Root refers to bruschette as "toast soaked with oil and garlic." It is the original garlic bread. When you have managed to find a truly extraordinary olive oil and an excellent coarse-textured loaf of peasant bread, treat yourself to bruschette. Cut the bread into slices a half inch thick. Grill until light grill marks appear, leaving the inside of the bread somewhat soft. Rub the hot bruschette with peeled garlic gloves and place on a plate. Drizzle over them fruity olive oil to taste, but enough to permeate the bruschette. In Spain, the grilled bread is rubbed with garlic and the cut side of a tomato for a delicious variation.

Crostini are lighter and more delicate than bruschette. They are generally topped with a spread such as Pesto di Olive (see page 276), or Chicken Liver Spread with Juniper Berries (see page 224), but they can be simply brushed with a light coating of garlic-flavored oil. They are also floated in soups. Take a good-quality thin Italian bread or French baguette and cut into half-inch slices. Arrange the bread rounds on a cookie sheet and place in a preheated 350° oven. Let the bread toast lightly just until the slices begin to color. The bread should not be hard-toasted all the way through.

Crostini can be made easily in the oven hours ahead in large quantities for cocktail parties. Just store the cooled crostini in a brown paper bag.

CAPERS

Capers grow wild along the Mediterranean. They are the unopened buds of a flowering shrub that thrives on arid land and in torrid heat. The buds are picked by hand before they blossom and are pickled in brine or packed in coarse salt. We use large capers when we want an assertive, distinct flavor that stands out as a separate component. Small capers are used more as a condiment to lend piquancy.

FRUIT DESSERTS

We think fruit is the natural ending to a meal. It is light, refreshes the eye and the palate, and for the calorie-conscious can be consumed with little or no guilt. The finest manifestation is fresh fruit of the season in a glass bowl filled with ice and water. Select the finest, sweetest fruit available for the fruit dessert recipes in this book, letting the seasons be your guide. The few non-fruit dessert recipes we offer, such as lightly sweetened fresh cheeses and granita, remain true to the spirit of natural, uncomplicated flavors.

GARLIC

We love to cook with garlic and can't imagine doing without it. Its distinctive flavor is intrinsic to much of what we enjoy eating. Look for fresh, young bulbs with firm cloves that haven't sprouted. Avoid yellowed, dried, or bruised cloves. Keep a store of minced garlic preserved in olive oil in the refrigerator in order to always have a ready supply of both minced garlic and garlic-flavored oil.

GRILLING

We look upon grilling as a serious alternative method of cooking, not just as a way to entertain on a hot summer day. There are two types of grills: those fired by coals and those using gas as the heat source. Using a charcoal grill gives you the opportunity to use aromatic wood charcoals which impart their unique flavor. However, a gas grill has the advantage of being more easily integrated into your daily life. Technology for kitchen gas and electric grills is much improved, making grilling possible year round. With gas grills heat is easily controlled, clean-up is minimal, the grill heats up rapidly, and results are excellent.

For charcoal grills we recommend wood charcoal or hard woods rather than petroleum charcoal briquets. Most wood charcoal burns hotter and longer. Hickory, a very hard wood, makes a long-lasting and strong-tasting charcoal. However, we use mesquite, which is readily available on the West Coast. Be aware that both hickory and mesquite can overpower delicate flavors. Wood charcoals can be purchased through mail-order sources listed in gourmet catalogs and magazines.

To control heat for cooking with charcoal, you must learn how to read the coals. Red-hot coals lightly covered with ash produce an intensely hot, fast-cooking heat; coals that have a medium coating of ash give off moderate heat; coals with a thick coating of white ash produce a low heat and are best for food that needs slow cooking or just warming. Coals placed close to one another produce a higher heat than coals spaced farther apart. Covering foods briefly while cooking adds an additional smoky flavor and raises the cooking temperature. Have a squirt bottle with a pin-point nozzle filled with water nearby to tame flare-ups. Use kindling to start your fire to avoid that splash of chemicals and telltale smell that used to signal the beginning of summer fun. As a special treat when grilling foods, throw a handful of aromatic herbs such as thyme or rosemary on the fire. The resulting perfumed smoke adds a special tang to meats and vegetables.

H E R B S

Wheat and beef, rice and fish are the
prose of food, herbs and spice are its poetry.

—*Waverley Root*

We like to think of herbs as food perfume. They infuse flavor directly into the flesh of food whether it be meats, vegetables or fruits. Sauces on the other hand are like clothes. Although they may enhance or make a dish more attractive, complementing the food's natural beauty, sauces basically cover up food. In the quest for eating more simply of less filling food, herbs are the flavoring agent of choice.

You will find that herbs are used abundantly throughout our recipes. Fresh herbs are always to be favored over dried, and once you begin to cook with them you will not be able to cook without them. The generous use of fresh herbs does not produce an overpowering flavor. In fact, fresh herbs may be viewed as a subgroup to leafy vegetables. When you become familiar with fresh herbs let your sense of taste be your guide in determining amounts. To wash herbs before using, such as basil or sage, it is usually necessary only to wipe the leaves with a damp towel. Do not drown them in water. If they are especially dirty, wash them by swishing in a bowl of cold water and shake to dry.

Our favorite herbs are parsley, basil, oregano, cilantro, mint, sage, rosemary, and thyme. In certain recipes whole sprigs are used; in others only the leaf is called for. With most of the herbs mentioned above it is simple to pluck the leaves from the tender stems. Rosemary and thyme, however, have woody stems. To remove rosemary leaves run two fingers along the length of the stem. It isn't necessary to remove the tiny thyme leaves one by one, a tedious process at best. Hold the bunch of thyme firmly in one hand and with a very sharp knife in the other, scrape downward, removing most of the tender leaves. The tender stems at the tip can be minced along with the leaves.

A word of caution when using dried herbs: While it is unnecessary to measure them in increments of $\frac{1}{8}$ and $\frac{1}{4}$ teaspoons, to use too much and too many can be overwhelming. In addition, be aware that their shelf life is limited. Purchase in small quantities. Make a habit of reviewing your spice shelf at least once a year, preferably twice. If dried herbs have become yellow or brown, or are markedly less pungent, discard them. The aromatic oils that impart flavor to food have fled. Crushing dried herbs between your fingers before adding them to foods allows the heat of your body to release their flavor and aroma. Some herbs dry more successfully than others. Sage, rosemary, thyme, oregano, mint, and even basil are quite effective in their dried state. Avoid dried parsley, chives, and mixed herbs such as "Italian seasonings" and "fines herbes." When buying dried herbs, always look for them in a form closest to their natural state, whole leaf or seed.

MARINATION

We believe in adding as much flavor to food as possible before cooking. To that end we make great use of dry and liquid marinades. A dry marinade is a mixture of herbs, salt, and sometimes garlic and pepper that is rubbed over and often stuffed into foods. In liquid marination herbs and spices are added to wine and/or oil, both to add flavor and ensure moistness.

OLIVE OIL

Like wine, the best olive oil comes from olives grown on farms, not from large factory-like operations. The gathering and pressing of olives in the Mediterranean countryside is almost a rite, following traditions and customs that go back centuries. Often farms that market their own wine, such as Antinori in Tuscany, also market oil from their trees. The harvest begins toward the end of autumn when the olives are about half ripe. They are either picked by hand, or tarps are spread on the ground to catch the fruit as it falls when the olive branches are beaten with sticks. The olives are collected and taken to the oil-press where they are squeezed between massive stones and reduced to an oily paste. This paste is put under tremendous pressure to bring forth the first and best oil, the extra-virgin.

There are four major classifications for olive oil: *Extra-virgin olive oil* comes, as we said, from the first pressing. The oil is dark green with a strong fruity or peppery taste of green olives. It is best used when the pure taste of raw oil is desired, on salads, in marinades, dressings, and on bruschette and crostini (see page 9). *Virgin olive oil* comes from the second pressing and is medium green to dark yellow in color, with a flavor that can range from lightly fruity to sweet and nutty. It, too, is excellent for all the above stated uses while being slightly more economical. We use it for frying when the oil remains a part of the dish, as in Fried Peppers (see page 161). *Pure olive oil* is produced by treating the previously pressed pulp with chemical solvents. It is light yellow in color and has a faint oily taste of olives. It is adequate for cooking. *Fine olive oil* is also produced by treating previously pressed pulp with solvents, but water is also added to extract the last of the oil from the pulp. It is the court of last resort for cooking.

Olive oil embodies all that is real, fragrant, and seductive about food and eating, and its connection to life. We consider olive oil to be the best cooking medium for the purposes of this book. As a flavoring agent it is unsurpassed, adding its own flavor and bouquet while enhancing the flavor of the foods with which it is paired. In the recipes that follow we refer to extra-virgin olive oil as "fruity olive oil." "Olive oil" refers to high-quality virgin or pure olive oil.

Some cooks recommend decanting olive oil that comes in cans; others think it is best to store the oil in the refrigerator. However, once you begin to appreciate the fine taste of really good-quality oil, the chances are you will use it up so rapidly that it will not have time to become rancid.

OLIVES

... black olives ... A taste older
than meat, older than wine.
A taste as old as cold water.

—Lawrence Durrell

Olives are basic to our style of eating. They aren't just an addition or an afterthought but are a food that is as satisfying to us as meat. The olives we eat and use in these recipes, both oil-cured and packed in brine, are imported and can be found in Italian and Greek delicatessens and specialty shops. Avoid domestic canned olives.

PASTA SALADS

Light and refreshing, yet satisfying, pasta salads are a beautiful, simple way to make a meal. We don't believe that these salads are simply endless variations of vegetables and meats tossed with a vinaigrette or mayonnaise dressing. Pasta salads need to be made with care. The pasta should be coated with a sauce which forms naturally from the juices of the ingredients, or on occasion a light dressing or "pesto." Key elements in making a good pasta salad are contrasting textures and fresh flavors to allow the honest flavor of the pasta to be appreciated.

We find imported Italian dried pasta is preferable to domestic dried or fresh pasta. It holds its shape, has better flavor, and remains al dente longer.

When preparing pasta ahead for cold pasta salads, toss the cooled, drained pasta with a tablespoon of olive oil to prevent sticking.

S A L T   A N D   P E P P E R

Salt and pepper seem to be givens, requiring no thought or choice. But these spices are crucial to every savory dish you cook.

Use coarse sea salt or kosher salt. Most brands are unadulterated, but you should check the labels to be sure. Because the product is pure, the salt flavor is stronger and less is needed. If the large grains of salt are not to your liking, crush them with a mortar and pestle, or buy fine-grained sea salt.

One of the wisest investments you can make is to acquire a high-quality pepper mill; there is no substitute for freshly ground black pepper, which we use exclusively. In many of our recipes we direct you to grind pepper over a finished dish just before serving. Do not consider this a cookbook reflex. The aromatic freshly ground pepper is an intrinsic part of the seasoning of these recipes.

S O U P S

We are fond of our cold soups and think they are special. They don't fit into the pattern of purées mixed with cream nor are they fruit based. We prefer full-bodied, hearty soups, closer in spirit to their hot counterparts. Many are served at room temperature rather than chilled, which allows the flavors to be fully appreciated.

Italians do not usually eat cold soups in the way we know them outside Italy. Only a few rustic soups served tepid or at room temperature would fall into this category. The cold soups authentic to Italy that we have included are Pappa al Pomodoro, Summer Minestrone with Pesto, and White Bean Soup with Rosemary. We have also included soups that remain true to the spirit of Italian food such as Roasted Red Pepper Soup and Two Endive Soup. Most of these soups have their roots in peasant culture and are made of staples which you are likely to have on hand. To these soups are added fruity olive oil, herb pastes, or fresh herb garnishes that enhance and enliven the already robust flavors.

S T A P L E S

Basic ingredients we like always to have on hand.

Extra-virgin olive oil
Good-quality virgin or pure olive oil
Good-quality red wine vinegar
Good-quality white wine vinegar
Balsamic vinegar
Garlic
Capers
Anchovies
Fresh supply of dried herbs

Dried red chile peppers
Coarse salt
Black peppercorns
Olives
Good mustard
Imported canned tomatoes
Imported Italian pasta
Long-grain white rice
Wild rice
Dry white beans
Italian Parmesan cheese

VINEGAR

The word vinegar comes from two French roots, *vin* meaning wine and *aigre* meaning sour. The best is now made commercially from wine in a two-stage manufacturing process, which first converts sugars to alcohol in a fermentation using yeast, and then converts the alcohol to "acetic acid" by introducing bacteria in the form of the "mother," a mass of special vinegar bacteria that often forms in bottles of red wine vinegar that are held for a while.

In this book vinegar is used as an intrinsic ingredient in meat and vegetable dishes. The quality of the finished dish rests on every ingredient in it, and for that reason it would be a pity to use jug vinegar on greens that have been lovingly chosen and carefully prepared. Good quality vinegar has a pleasing acid odor that is neither strong nor offensive. The color should be that of the wine from which it was made. It should be transparent, a quality sometimes difficult to discern with opaque and colored bottles. White wine vinegar should be more or less a straw yellow color.

It is possible to create an almost infinite variety of tastes with either red or white wine vinegar. Simply add a preferred herb or spice to a sterilized glass container of vinegar, and cork. Some choices are basil, rosemary, mint, hot peppers (whole or flaked), onion, garlic, capers, or black peppercorns. Leave the bottle on the windowsill where it is exposed to the sun. As time goes by the herbal flavor will intensify. Herbal vinegars are inexpensive and beautiful as gifts, but save some for yourself to brighten a salad, vegetable, fruit, or cold meat. To avoid tiring of these flavored vinegars, use them alternately with a good plain wine vinegar. When cooking with vinegar or dressing a salad, use vinegar sparingly; with a good-quality vinegar, a little goes a long way.

Of all the specialty vinegars produced around the world, the best to our minds is aceto balsamico, or balsamic vinegar, produced in Modena, Italy. This incredibly flavorful vinegar is produced by adding the must of the grape to the barrels that store the vinegar. The ensuing process of deacidifying the vinegar takes approximately twenty-five years during which the vinegar is transferred from red oak kegs to chestnut, mulberry, and juniper, one after another. The resulting dense vinegar with its characteristic deep reddish-brown color and sweet-sour taste bears traces of the flavor of each of the woods in which it has aged. In Italy very special examples of balsamic vinegar are sold in pharmacies by the gram and are quite costly. They are used medicinally and taken as a digestive. We love balsamic vinegar simply poured over ripe berries, served in the cavity of a fresh avocado, or as a treat over sliced ripe tomatoes with basil. It is also marvelous to use when deglazing pans for sauces.

When buying vegetables and fruits respect the seasons. The arrival of tender asparagus in early spring or the appearance of real tomatoes in summer is cause for celebration. Although produce is now shipped to us from all over the world and nectarines may appear in your market in the middle of winter, it is important to relearn when certain vegetables and fruits are in season. You will be rewarded with better flavor, better prices, and most importantly you will feel that connection with nature that the supermarket experience dulls. We urge you to seek out specialty food stores, ethnic markets, and roadside produce stands where you will find better quality and wider variety.

One last request: be demanding. You don't have to be limited to the foodstuffs immediately available to you. Supermarkets are becoming more aware of eating trends and are responding with better quality and selection. For example, at one time fresh basil was nonexistent in markets here in Los Angeles. It is now widely available. A merchant will always respond when there is an audience large enough to support a special product, so ask your local market to carry special items. It is also worth the time to find a good fishmonger and butcher who will be responsive to your special needs. There is no reason for you, the cook, to spend your time boning a whole chicken when a professional will gladly do the job.

M E N U S

Sharing a meal is a good excuse for people to come together—whether it is the family dinner at the end of the day or when an unusually beautiful day beckons you outdoors with picnic basket in hand. Sometimes food is most memorable when spontaneously prepared to share with friends and family. Because of its simplicity, much of our food lends itself to more impromptu dining. In its simplicity, however, lies an inherent elegance which allows you to compose menus for more formal occasions as well. We include a sampling of menus to illustrate some of the possibilities. These menus are meant to be your inspiration and are not rigidly prescribed by any means. Those recipes marked with an asterisk do not appear in this book. Let your style and imagination guide you.

Early Fall Barbecue
Grilled Stuffed Wild Mushrooms
Roasted Red Onions in Balsamic Vinegar
Sweet and Sour Squash
Grilled Flank Steak
Green Salad*
Assorted Fruit in Season

A Seafood Birthday Dinner
Crab in Lemon Dressing
Mussels in White Wine and Garlic
Insalata di Calamari
Gelo di Melone
Espresso

New Year's Eve Supper for 2
Insalata Russa on Radicchio Leaves Garnished
with Cornichons and Lemon Slices
Lobster and Roasted Red Peppers
Tea Granita and Peaches Steeped in Cognac

Saturday Picnic Grill
Prosciutto
Escalivada
Bay-Scented Pork Liver Spiedini
Watercress Salad* with Garlic Vinaigrette
Pears with Gorgonzola and Goat Cheese

Sunday in the Park
Ricotta al Forno
Parsley Frittata
Tomato and Mozzarella Salad with
Capers and Oregano
Artichokes in Tomato Sauce
Country-Style Rigatoni Salad
Assorted Fruit in Season

Dinner with Friends and Family
Grissini
Oil-Cured Black Olives
Tender Green Beans* in Garlic Vinaigrette
Grattó di Patate
Whole Roasted Tomatoes with
Basil-Flavored Olive Oil
Oranges

Formal Family Dinner
Chicken Liver Spread with Juniper
Berries Served with Crostini
Deep-Fried Baby Zucchini and Zucchini Blossoms*
Turkey Breast with Herb Butter
Kale and Black Olives
Caprese with Arugola and Belgian Endive
Figs Poached in Red Wine

Rustic Country Lunch
Spicy Green Olives with Rosemary
Grissini
Timballo di Melanzone
Simple Green Salad
Cherries and Grapes

Dinner for a Winter Evening
Cauliflower in Salsa Verde
Arista
Pearl Onions Braised in Orange Juice
Insalata di Riso Selvatico
Persimmons

Easter Celebration
Hard-Cooked Eggs and Whole Basil Leaves Served
with Coarse Salt and Freshly Ground Pepper
Veal Roast Flavored with Rosemary and Garlic
Spinach Croquettes
Asparagus and Carrot Julienne
Tomato Halves with Pesto di Olive
Strawberries with Zabaglione-Flavored
Whipped Cream

Roman Lunch
Simple Asparagus with Olive Oil and Lemon
Pollo Tonnato
Tomato Halves with Parsley Sauce
Caramelized Oranges

Lunch for 1
Artichoke Roman-Style
Carpaccio with Arugola and Parmesan
Ricotta and Crystallized Honey

Tuscan Dinner Alfresco
Pinzimonio
Pappa al Pomodoro
Florentine Grilled Steak
Insalata Composta
Biscotti and Vin Santo

Dinner for 8
Caprini Piccante
Zuppa di Fagioli
Grilled Butterflied Leg of Lamb with
Rosemary Vinaigrette
Simple Artichokes with Anchovy Dressing
Mushroom Salad with Mustard Vinaigrette*
Pink Honeydew Melon

Sunday Dinner for 6
Bread-Stuffed Artichokes
Insalata di Mare
Caramelized Figs

July Fourth Lunch for 20
Grilled Tuna with Tomato Garnish
Ricotta Frittata
Grilled Baby Zucchini*
Lettuce Salad with Extra-Virgin
Olive Oil and Vinegar
Marinated Eggplant
Raw Baby Carrots
Raw Yellow and Black Bell Peppers
Orange, Onion, and Mint Salad
Penne alla Caprese
Watermelon and Wine

Dinner for 4
Trout Marinated with Sage
Wild and White Rice Salad
Roasted Pepper Salad with Basil
Tomato, Avocado, and Red Onion Salad
Red Flame Grapes

Concert Picnic Dinner
Minestra al Limone
Marinated Roasted Red and Yellow
Peppers with Oregano
Veal-Stuffed Quail Tart
Fresh Italian Prunes in Port

Breakfast for 2
Pasta Frittata
Orange and Fennel Salad

Dinner for 4
Avocado and Grapefruit Salad
Marinated Cooked Beef
Spinach with Anchovies
Yellow Bell Peppers in Vinegar,
Sugar, and Oregano
Peaches Stuffed with Amaretti,
Almonds, and Chocolate

Country Picnic for 80
Grilled Sausages*
Polenta*
Rosemary Chicken
Fried Peppers
Panzanella
Caprese
Torta Rustica
Herb-stuffed Eggplant
Zucchini in Carpione
Mushrooms with Mint and Tomato
Prosciutto
Grapes, Figs, and Strawberries
Country Breads

A Grilled Quail Dinner
Spicy Oyster Salad
Thyme-Scented Quail
Grilled Green or Golden Zucchini
Carrot Salad with Gorgonzola Cream
The Maestro's Berries

soups

Each of the following cold soups is simple and inexpensive, and most can be made with water. However, there are times when the more full-bodied flavor of a chicken or vegetable stock is desired. When the mood strikes, we recommend preparing several quarts of each and freezing for convenience. If making stock is not your vision of weekend entertainment, canned broth is an acceptable substitute. Canned broth tends to be highly salted, so take care in the amount of salt you add. We do not recommend using bouillon cubes or consommé. Remember to thoroughly skim chicken broth of all fat before using in the soup recipes. Congealed fat floating atop a beautiful soup is not very appetizing.

CHICKEN BROTH

1 medium stewing chicken, or
    backs, necks, and wings of
    3 chickens
3 quarts of water
1 onion, peeled and cut into
    quarters
2 carrots, peeled and coarsely
    chopped
2 celery stalks, washed and
    coarsely chopped

1 bay leaf
1 fresh sage leaf, or ¼
    teaspoon dried sage leaves
2 fresh basil leaves, or ½
    teaspoon dried basil
    leaves
Sprig of fresh thyme or pinch
    of dried thyme leaves
Freshly ground pepper

Place the chicken and all the other ingredients in a large pot. Bring to a boil, skimming off the scum that rises to the top. When there is no more scum, lower the heat and simmer, uncovered, for 1 to 2 hours. Strain the broth and refrigerate for later use. When the fat congeals on top of the cold broth, carefully lift it off and discard. *Makes 1½ quarts.*

VEGETABLE BROTH

2 pounds mixed vegetables in
    season
3–4 tablespoons butter or olive
    oil

3 quarts water
1 tablespoon coarse salt
Small handful fresh herbs

Wash and clean the vegetables carefully and cut into a medium dice. Sauté them in either butter or olive oil in a large saucepan until softened. Add the water, salt, and any fresh or dried herbs you may have on hand such as parsley, basil, thyme, or summer savory. Bring to a boil. Lower the heat and simmer, uncovered, for 1 hour. Strain the broth and set aside in the refrigerator for soup making. *Makes 1½ quarts.*

POTATO-TOMATO SOUP WITH SAGE

This soup is surprisingly light and refreshing although one might assume otherwise. The small amount of cream lends a velvet texture and smooths out the soup. Blending the tomatoes with potatoes gives this soup a lovely pink color and a delicious taste.

1½ pounds potatoes, peeled and coarsely chopped
10 garlic cloves, peeled
3 tablespoons fresh sage leaves, stems removed, or 1 tablespoon dried sage leaves, crumbled
2 bay leaves
1 onion, peeled and coarsely chopped

1 tablespoon coarse salt
4 cups water
2 large ripe tomatoes, peeled, seeded, and chopped (see note)
2 tablespoons olive oil
¼ cup heavy cream
Fresh sage leaves for garnish

Combine the potatoes, garlic, herbs, onion, salt, and water in a large saucepan. Bring to a boil, then lower the heat and simmer until the potatoes are very tender, about 10 to 12 minutes after water comes to the boil.

Sauté the tomatoes in the olive oil in a skillet over high heat until the tomato juices thicken. Set aside. When the potato mixture is ready, purée together with the tomatoes in a blender or food processor. You may need to process the ingredients in 2 batches. When the mixture is smooth, pour it into a bowl and stir in the cream. Chill the soup and serve in bowls with a fresh sage leaf as garnish. *Serves 4 to 6.*

NOTE: TO PEEL AND SEED TOMATOES

Drop the tomatoes into boiling water for 5 to 10 seconds, just enough to loosen the skin; they should not cook. The object is to keep them as intact as possible. Remove from the boiling water and cool them immediately under cold running water to stop the cooking and facilitate handling. Cut out the stem and peel off the skin. Treat the peeled tomatoes carefully. Cut them in half crosswise, and with your finger carefully scoop out the seeds. The tomatoes are now ready to be used in a recipe calling for peeled and seeded tomatoes.

When only a few tomatoes need to be peeled, it is faster to roast them lightly over a gas flame, rather than going to the bother of boiling a pot of water. Impale each tomato on a fork through the stem end and place it directly in the flame. Turn it until it is lightly charred here and there. Remember that the purpose of charring the tomato is to peel, not to cook the tomato. The job is done very quickly.

PAPPA AL POMODORO

Among the most satisfying soups we have tasted and one of the simplest is Pappa al Pomodoro. In the almost monastic surroundings of the Florentine restaurant Coco Lezzone, this traditional Tuscan dish reaches sublime heights. The importance of using olive oil of the highest possible quality with a strong fruity flavor cannot be overemphasized. If you do not have access to good country bread, do not attempt the recipe. The word "pappa" literally translated means mush and usually refers to baby food. It would be a lucky and sophisticated baby to be fed a dish of Pappa al Pomodoro!

2 garlic cloves, peeled and chopped
¾ cup fruity olive oil
1 bunch fresh sage leaves, stems removed, or 1–2 tablespoons dried sage leaves
1½ pounds day-old country bread, cut into small thin slices
1½ pounds ripe tomatoes, peeled, seeded, and puréed, or a large can (28 ounces) tomatoes, puréed with their liquid
Coarse salt and freshly ground pepper to taste
Water
Grated Parmesan cheese for garnish

Sauté the garlic briefly in the oil in a saucepan on a high flame. Add the sage and bread to the pan. Mix with a wooden spoon until the bread turns golden to medium brown. Add the tomato purée, salt, and pepper. Bring to a boil and boil for 5 minutes, stirring constantly. Add just enough cold water to cover the bread-tomato mixture. Bring to a simmer. Cover and cook over a low flame, stirring often, for at least 30 minutes or until the "pappa" achieves its unique consistency, somewhere between thick and runny; it should grab the spoon. Serve the soup tepid and pass Parmesan cheese. *Serves 4 to 6.*

Z U P P A   D I   F A G I O L I
w h i t e   b e a n   s o u p

To add texture to the soup, reserve 1 cup or so of whole cooked beans and stir them into the rest of the bean purée. A large bowl of this satisfying soup served with a salad makes a simple, delicious luncheon. Have a cruet of intensely fruity olive oil on the table to drizzle into the soup.

*1 pound dried small white
    beans*

Water

*3 sprigs fresh rosemary, or 2
    teaspoons dried rosemary
    leaves, crumbled*

*1 large onion, peeled and
    coarsely chopped*

*3 tablespoons plus 2 teaspoons
    olive oil*

*1 garlic clove, peeled and
    minced*

*4 tomatoes, peeled, seeded,
    and diced fine*

Coarse salt to taste

*2 lasagne noodles, broken into
    irregular shapes, about 2
    inches*

Fruity olive oil for garnish

Wash the beans and discard any discolored ones. Place the beans in a heavy pot and add 2½ times as much water. Bring to a boil, lower the heat, and let simmer for 5 minutes. Cover the pot, turn off heat, and let sit for 1 hour. Uncover the pot and bring back to a boil. Lower the heat to a simmer and add the rosemary and onion. Let simmer until the beans are tender, adding additional boiling water if necessary. Cooking time should be about 1 hour, depending on the age of the beans. Drain the beans, reserving the cooking liquid. Reserve 1 cup beans to add at the end. Discard fresh rosemary sprigs.

Heat the 3 tablespoons olive oil in a large skillet. Add the garlic, beans, and tomatoes. Add 1 cup of the reserved bean cooking liquid and salt to taste. Cook over medium heat just until tomatoes soften into the beans. Purée the beans and tomatoes in a food processor or blender, in batches if necessary, adding more reserved cooking liquid as needed to bring the soup to a proper consistency; it should be thick enough to coat a spoon. Stir in the reserved 1 cup beans. Cool in the refrigerator.

Meanwhile, cook broken lasagne noodles in an abundant amount of boiling salted water until al dente. Drain the noodles and rinse under cold running water until they feel cool to the touch. Place in a small bowl and mix with the 2 teaspoons olive oil to prevent sticking. Serve the soup at room temperature. When ready to serve, stir in the noodles. Pass more olive oil at the table. *Serves 6 to 8.*

SUMMER MINESTRONE WITH PESTO

Since minestrone has the reputation of being a hot and hearty winter soup, eating it at room temperature is a revelation. The fresh, uncooked flavor of the basil and garlic brings the wealth of vegetable tastes into relief.

2 ounces prosciutto (about 4 slices), chopped
1 onion, peeled and chopped
2 tablespoons chopped fresh parsley
4 tablespoons olive oil
1 small savoy cabbage, shredded and chopped
1 potato, peeled and diced
1 cup canned tomatoes with juice, preferably imported
¼ pound tender green beans, cut into ½-inch pieces

1 carrot, peeled and diced
2 celery stalks, diced
2 medium zucchini, diced
4 cups chicken broth
1 cup freshly cooked or canned white beans plus ½ cup of their liquid
½ cup basmati rice, or other long-grain white rice
Pesto, 1 teaspoon per serving (see page 101)
Fresh basil leaves cut into strips for garnish (optional)

Sauté the prosciutto, onion, and parsley in the olive oil in a large stockpot until the onion colors and softens. Add the cabbage and toss until it loses some volume. Add the remaining vegetables. Toss to coat with the oil. Add the chicken broth and beans with their liquid, and simmer, uncovered, for about 35 minutes or until the vegetables are cooked and the liquid has thickened.

Meanwhile, cook the rice in an abundant amount of boiling salted water for 12 minutes or until al dente. Drain. Add to the soup a few minutes before all the vegetables are finished cooking. The soup will be thick. Let the soup cool to room temperature. To serve, ladle the soup into bowls. Swirl 1 teaspoon pesto into each bowl. Garnish with strips of fresh basil, if available. The pesto should not be completely mixed into the soup, but left in swirls and eaten that way. If mixed in the pesto muddies the fresh flavors of the soup. *Serves 4 to 6.*

ZUPPA DI ZUCCA
butternut squash soup

Squash gives this pretty soup body. The apples and onions lend a touch of sweetness.

½ pound butternut or other
    yellow squash, peeled,
    seeded, and cut into small
    dice
½ pound tart apples, peeled,
    cored, and cut into small
    dice
½ pound yellow onions, peeled
    and cut into small dice
2 tablespoons butter
1 tablespoon olive oil

2–4 cups chicken broth
2 sprigs fresh rosemary, or 2
    teaspoons dried rosemary
    leaves, crumbled
2 sprigs fresh marjoram, or 1
    teaspoon dried marjoram
    leaves, crumbled
Coarse salt and freshly ground
    pepper to taste
Fresh rosemary sprigs and/or
    marjoram sprigs for
    garnish

Cook the diced squash, apples, and onions in the butter and oil in a large skillet over low heat until the fruits and vegetables are soft. Add 1 cup of the chicken broth and the herbs, season and continue cooking for 5 minutes. Purée the mixture in a food processor or blender, adding enough additional chicken broth to give desired consistency. Strain through sieve to remove the herbs. Refrigerate. Serve chilled, garnished with fresh herbs. *Serves 6.*

ROASTED RED PEPPER SOUP

The roasting of the peppers adds a grilled, smoky dimension to the flavor of this vivid, bright orange-red soup with garnishes of fragrant freshly torn basil leaves and the sweet citrus tang of paper-thin slices of lemon. Serve with Bruschette (page 9).

4 meaty red bell peppers, roasted, peeled, cored, and seeded (see page 94)
2 cups imported Italian canned tomatoes, seeded and drained
3 tablespoons olive oil
2 cloves garlic, peeled and finely minced
3 cups defatted chicken stock
Salt and freshly ground black pepper
Basil leaves for garnish
Paper-thin slices of lemon for garnish

Purée three of the peppers and all the tomatoes in a food processor or blender until finely textured but not completely smooth. Cut the remaining pepper into thin julienne strips and set aside.

Gently heat the olive oil and garlic. When the garlic releases its fragrance, after about two minutes, stir in the puréed pepper and tomato mixture. Add the chicken stock, bring to a boil and simmer for 15 minutes. Season with salt and pepper to taste.

Let the soup cool, then cover and chill in the refrigerator. To serve, ladle soup into bowls. Tear basil leaves into pieces and scatter over soup. Float a lemon slice in each bowl. *Serves 4.*

MINESTRA FRESCA

This wonderfully fresh-tasting tomato soup infused with the heady perfume of fresh marjoram should be served very cold with the best available grissini wrapped in beautiful pale pink, paper-thin slices of prosciutto. Accompany with a chilled glass of Chiaretto, an Italian rosé.

2 pounds ripe tomatoes, peeled and seeded
2 tablespoons olive oil
1 small clove garlic, peeled and finely minced
2 cups defatted chicken stock

Salt and freshly ground black pepper
2 teaspoons minced fresh marjoram
Fresh marjoram leaves for garnish

Purée the tomatoes in a blender or food processor until finely textured but not completely smooth. Gently heat olive oil and garlic in a medium sized saucepan. When garlic becomes fragrant, after about 2 minutes, stir in the tomatoes. Add the chicken stock. Bring to a boil, then reduce the heat and simmer for 8 to 10 minutes, or until the tomatoes are just cooked through. Correct seasonings, adding salt and pepper as necessary. (The stock may provide enough salt.) Cool. Stir in fresh marjoram, then cover and chill for 2 hours. To serve, garnish with fresh marjoram leaves. *Serves 4.*

TWO ENDIVE SOUP

Using bitter greens in soup is a longstanding Italian culinary tradition. The combined flavor of these two endives makes this beautiful cool soup even more refreshing.

2 tablespoons olive oil
¼ small onion, peeled and
*   minced*
½ celery stalk, peeled and cut
*   crosswise into thin slices*
1 garlic clove, peeled and
*   minced*
1 small head endive lettuce,
*   washed thoroughly and*
*   tough outer leaves*
*   discarded*

7 cups chicken stock **or**
*   vegetable broth* **or** *water*
Salt and freshly ground black
*   pepper to taste*
¼ cup long-grain white rice
1 head Belgian endive,
*   medium sized, leaves cut*
*   lengthwise into ¼-inch*
*   julienne strips*
1 tablespoon minced parsley
*   for garnish*

Heat the olive oil in a large saucepan and stir in the onion, celery, and garlic. Cook gently over low heat until the vegetables begin to soften. Meanwhile, slice the endive lettuce into thin strips. When the celery mixture is ready, add the endive lettuce. Stir so that the lettuce leaves are coated with the oil. Add the broth or water and salt and pepper to taste. Bring the liquid to a simmer over medium heat. Add the rice and cook until soft yet still firm. Remove from the heat and cool to room temperature.

After the soup cools, stir the julienne of Belgian endive into cooled soup and correct the seasoning. Ladle the soup into individual bowls and garnish with minced parsley. *Serves 4 to 6.*

MINESTRA AL LIMONE
lemon soup with zucchini

A classic, astringent summer soup made more substantial by the addition of zucchini and orzo.

2 quarts chicken broth
Coarse salt
4 eggs
Juice of 2 lemons
2 small zucchini, trimmed

½ cup of orzo (rice-shaped pasta) (optional)
Olive oil
1 lemon, thinly sliced for garnish

Bring the chicken broth to a boil in a large saucepan. Add salt to taste. Meanwhile, beat the eggs in a medium bowl with a whisk or in an electric mixer until thick and frothy. Slowly add the lemon juice, beating constantly. Slowly add 2 cups of hot broth, still beating constantly to prevent the eggs from curdling. Stir the egg-lemon mixture into the remainder of the hot chicken broth. Let cool and refrigerate.

Either grate the zucchini in a food processor or cut into julienne strips. Blanch the zucchini in boiling salted water for 45 seconds just to set the color and remove the raw taste. Quickly drain zucchini in a sieve and run under cold water until cool to the touch. Set aside in refrigerator.

Cook the orzo in an abundant amount of boiling salted water until al dente, tender yet still firm to the bite, about 10 minutes. Drain in a sieve and run under cold water until cool. Drain and set aside. If making orzo more than half an hour ahead, place in a bowl, add 1 teaspoon olive oil to prevent the pasta from sticking to itself, and refrigerate until needed. To serve, mix the zucchini and orzo together with the soup. Serve chilled. Garnish with lemon slices, if desired. *Serves 6 to 8.*

GARLIC SOUP

Boiled garlic has a mellow, nutty flavor that permeates this comforting cold soup.

*½ small onion, peeled and
    minced*
*6 garlic cloves, peeled and
    coarsely chopped*
2 tablespoons olive oil
*1 medium baking potato,
    peeled and sliced*

4 cups chicken broth
1 cup light cream
2 tablespoons sour cream
*Coarse salt and freshly ground
    pepper to taste*

Briefly sauté the onion and garlic in the oil in a medium saucepan. Add the potato and chicken broth. Bring to a boil. Lower the heat and simmer until the potato and garlic are soft. Purée the mixture in a blender or food processor. Pour the soup into a bowl. Place in the refrigerator to cool. To serve, stir in the light cream and sour cream. Season with salt and pepper. *Serves 4.*

MINESTRA ALL'INSALATA

A fresh colorful garden salad turned soup.

6 large tomatoes, peeled, seeded, and finely chopped

1 small red onion, peeled and finely diced

1 hot-house cucumber, peeled, seeded, and finely diced

2 large red bell peppers, peeled, stemmed, seeded, and finely diced

4 large garlic cloves, peeled and lightly crushed

1 cup cooked long-grain white rice

2 cups water

¼ cup fruity olive oil

1 tablespoon red wine vinegar

Cayenne pepper to taste

Coarse salt and freshly ground pepper to taste

Finely chopped fresh basil for garnish

Combine all ingredients in a large bowl and stir well. Cover and refrigerate until very cold. Remove garlic cloves. Correct seasonings, adding more vinegar, cayenne, salt or pepper as needed. Garnish with basil. *Serves 4.*

salads

Radicchio, Mâche, and Arugola

Radicchio is an extraordinarily dramatic head lettuce. The first time we saw the amazing vegetable was in an open-air market in Northern Italy. An Italian friend laughed when we asked why the sellers had taken all the stems off the "gorgeous red flowers." He explained that the "flowers" were heads of winter lettuce. Cultivated in Treviso and Verona, Italy, where it is a traditional Christmas dish, radicchio is now available as an import nearly year round.

Characterized by a full rounded head, radicchio is the size of Bibb lettuce, with compact, curled leaves. The color ranges from a dark magenta to light pink, and often the leaves are boldly streaked with white or mottled with small white speckles. Radicchio has a crisp texture and a slightly bitter taste resembling that of Belgian endive. Just one or two well-placed leaves of radicchio used as a garnish can dramatically enhance a simple plate presentation.

Another green to make its retail appearance in markets over the past couple of years is mâche, a member of the chicory family. Known as songino in Italian and lamb's lettuce in English, mâche is the term used most frequently on restaurant menus and in the markets. It grows wild in European meadows at the beginning of spring where it is a lamb's favorite treat. Like Belgian endive, mâche is available throughout the fall, winter, and spring seasons. It has small, thumb-size oval leaves that grow from a central heart. The plants are harvested at an early stage of development when they are sweet, extremely tender, and medium to light green in color. Its buttery taste, delicate texture, and small unique leaf size and shape make mâche a natural complement to more strongly flavored greens. It is also beautiful as a garnish when the leaves are left attached to the core.

Arugola (rugola in Italy and rocket in England) is dark green with long rocket-shaped leaves with jagged edges. Grown in Florida and available in the New York area for many years, arugola has become increasingly popular over the past few years. In its natural state, the plant grows like dandelion or mustard greens, and it was traditionally gathered as a wild green from the fields.

Arugola has an intense, pleasing aroma and a strong, spicy flavor with a slightly bitter finish, a pronounced taste with more character than either radicchio or mâche.

When choosing these lettuces from the produce stands, remember that most of them have traveled great distances to get to the United States. Choose carefully. Peek inside the head of radicchio to be sure the inside leaves are as beautiful as the outside ones. The heads are often closed tight and when opened at home can reveal themselves to be less than perfect. Mâche and arugola are more prone to wilting than radicchio, which is a sturdier vegetable. Choose the freshest and most crisp appearing plants. Avoid arugola with yellow spots as these leaves will soon wilt. Use the lettuces as soon as possible after purchase, ideally the same day. If you must store them for a few days, there are ways to prolong the crispness of these delicate plants. Wash the radicchio so that water flushes out the core; break the heads open if necessary. The vegetable can then be wrapped in a dish towel and put into a plastic bag. Arugola can be stored submerged in water. Mâche, however, is very delicate. We have had some success keeping the plant for one or two days by wrapping the unwashed bunches in a damp paper towel.

The salad which follows makes good use of the contrasts in texture, color, and taste of radicchio, arugola, and mâche.

INSALATA ELEVATA
elevated mixed salad

1 head radicchio
2 heads limestone lettuce, or 1
    head butter lettuce
1 bunch arugola

½ pound mâche
1 recipe Simple Virgin
    Dressing (see page 263)

Break apart the radicchio and limestone lettuces to separate the leaves. Trim the arugola stems. Cut the mâche free from its core. Wash all the lettuce and dry by rolling it in a towel or using a salad spinner. Toss all the greens together in a salad bowl with the Simple Virgin Dressing. *Serves 4 to 6.*

SALAD PARTY À LA GIANNI VERSACE

We are not sure where our memory ends and imagination begins, but we were inspired reading about a party given by Gianni Versace, the well-known Italian fashion designer. Baskets of fresh lettuce leaves along with condiments were served buffet style, each guest selecting and seasoning his or her own salad. This salad party can be as simple or as exuberant as you want. Just do not stray too far from the suggestions outlined below. For a salad bar par excellence, serve with assorted cheeses and breads.

Choose from the following lettuces and greens:

Arugola

Radicchio

Romaine

Butter

Mâche

Watercress

Belgian endive

Escarole

Curly endive

Sorrel

Red leaf

Spinach

Dandelion

Choose from the following vegetables:

Tomatoes

Carrots

Cucumbers

Red onion

Fennel

Celery heart

Choose from the following fresh herbs:

Basil leaves   **Tarragon sprigs**
Mint leaves   **Chives**
Flat-leaf parsley

Set out cruets of fruity olive oil, excellent red wine vinegar, balsamic vinegar, and small lemons cut in half and seeded.

Wash all the ingredients well. Separate and detach leaves and trim stems of lettuces and greens when necessary. Discard any bruised leaves or tough outer leaves. Wrap in tea towels and chill until needed. Peel carrots and cucumbers. Remove skin from onion. Trim fennel bulb of tough stalks and remove bruised outer layers. Place cleaned vegetables along with the celery heart in lightly moistened tea towels or plastic bags and put in the refrigerator.

Before serving, cut tomatoes into wedges, grate carrots, cut cucumbers into rounds, thinly slice red onion, cut fennel into slivers, and cut celery hearts into small pieces. Place lettuces in separate baskets, leaving smaller leaves whole and tearing larger leaves into bite-size pieces. Put prepared vegetables into separate bowls. Place fresh herbs in small bowls. Set out the cruets of olive oil and vinegars, and the cut lemons. Put out small dishes of coarse salt with little spoons and a pepper mill. Offer a variety of cheeses such as imported Parmesan, gorgonzola, and fontina in large chunks and balls of fresh mozzarella. Serve with coarse country breads and grissini. Serve carafes of simple wines—a chilled, lemony, dry white wine and a light, dry red wine. Follow with a selection of seasonal fruits such as cherries and apricots in large glass bowls with ice cubes and water to keep the fruit chilled.

PINZIMONIO

A celebration of tender, seasonal vegetables. We find this Italian way with raw vegetables a superb beginning to a meal. Place a small dish of extra-virgin olive oil next to each person. Pass coarse salt for seasoning the oil and have a pepper mill on the table. Provide a selection of raw vegetables for dipping, a restrained few or a large assortment. Choose whatever is freshest and most tempting.

Set these out on the table:

Fruity olive oil
Coarse salt
Pepper mill

Choose from the following vegetables:

*Artichokes—very tender, small artichokes cut in half or
    quartered and rubbed with lemon*
Carrots—very young, thin carrots, peeled and left whole
Celery hearts—stalks detached and leaves left on
*Radishes—small, unblemished, with root end trimmed and a
    few leaves left on if very fresh looking*
*Fennel—bruised outer stalks removed and bulb cut into
    quarters or eighths, depending on size*
Fava beans—shelled
Radicchio—leaves detached
Asparagus—very thin stalks, tough ends trimmed
Hearts of romaine—leaves detached
Red and yellow bell peppers—cored, seeded, and cut into strips

PANZANELLA
bread salad

This peasant specialty from Tuscany requires above all good country bread. The bread traditionally used is a large, round, coarse loaf baked in a brick oven. A loaf of French or Italian bread of high quality is an acceptable substitute. In Tuscan dialect Panzanella means "little swamp," an apt description of the juice-soaked bread.

½ loaf day-old country bread, or French or Italian bread
2 tomatoes, peeled, seeded, and cut into ½-inch dice
1–2 tablespoons capers
½ cup fruity olive oil
¼ cup red wine vinegar
Coarse salt and freshly ground pepper to taste

3 cucumbers, peeled, halved, seeded, and cut into ½-inch dice
½ small red onion, peeled and thinly sliced
1 bell pepper, red, yellow, or green, cored, seeded, and cut lengthwise into very thin strips

Cut the bread into ½-inch-thick slices and remove the crusts. Set aside. Mix together in a bowl the tomatoes, capers, oil, vinegar, salt, and pepper. In a wide, shallow bowl or large platter make a layer of bread slices. Scatter the cucumbers, onion, and bell pepper strips over the bread. Pour a ladleful of the tomato mixture over the bread and vegetables. Continue layering until all the ingredients are used up, ending with vegetables and tomato mixture. Set the dish aside at room temperature or in the refrigerator for at least 1 hour. It is important for the bread to absorb the liquid from the vegetables and tomato mixture. If the dish seems too dry, sprinkle on more oil and vinegar. Panzanella can be made a day ahead. *Serves 6.*

ESCAROLE WITH WALNUTS, CELERY, AND PARMESAN

This winter salad is beautiful in shades of pale yellow and gold, and the dressing adds tang to an already flavorful dish. Salads are often overlooked in winter, but greens are always available to put together a salad characteristic of the season. The tough outer leaves of the escarole can be reserved for cooking later in olive oil and lemon juice (see page 152).

2 heads escarole
½ cup thinly sliced celery heart
¼ pound Parmesan cheese, cut into thin slivers

⅓ cup broken walnuts
½ recipe Anchovy Dressing (see page 264)

Wash the escarole and remove the tough outer leaves. Tear the remaining tender inner leaves into bite-size pieces and combine in a salad bowl with the celery, Parmesan cheese, and walnuts. Toss with the Anchovy Dressing. *Serves 4.*

ORANGE, ONION, AND MINT SALAD

The glossy color of the oranges sends us. Sometimes we omit the olives and mint and add peeled and sliced kiwis. We would rather serve this than a fruit compote for a brunch salad.

3–4 navel oranges
½ small red onion, peeled and cut into paper-thin slices
1 tablespoon coarsely chopped fresh mint leaves

1 tablespoon oil-cured black olives, pits removed, cut in half
1 tablespoon olive oil

Peel the oranges, removing as much of the white pith as possible. Cut the peeled oranges crosswise into ¼-inch-thick slices. Arrange the orange slices on a platter. Either alternate the orange slices with the onion slices, or separate the onion slices into rings and scatter on top of the oranges. Sprinkle the chopped mint and pitted olives over the oranges and onions. Just before serving, sprinkle with olive oil. *Serves 4 to 8.*

FENNEL, GREEN BEAN, AND OLIVE SALAD

Raw fennel with its light, licorice flavor and crisp texture is such a treat that we use it often when it is available. It is wonderful alone, cut into slivers and drizzled with a little olive oil and lemon juice. A unique presentation in Palermo adds fresh citron rind to the slivered fennel. In Italy fennel is sometimes served after the meal as you would fruit to refresh the palate. With this salad serve crostini (see Page 9) rubbed with garlic.

1 pound tender green beans, trimmed
1 large fennel bulb (about 1 pound)
¼ cup fruity olive oil
3 tablespoons lemon juice
1 canned flat anchovy fillet, minced

1 garlic clove, peeled and crushed
Coarse salt to taste
¼ cup oil-cured black olives, pitted and quartered
Freshly ground pepper

If green beans are large, cut them in half lengthwise. Tough old beans should not be used in salads. Blanch the green beans in an abundant amount of boiling salted water until they are tender yet still crisp, about 10 minutes. Drain and refresh under cold running water. Shake dry. Trim the stalks off the fennel bulb and cut away any bruised, discolored, or tough outer leaves. Cut the fennel bulb in half lengthwise. Trim the root end and cut out the core at the base of the bulb. Slice the fennel lengthwise into thin strips. To make the dressing, combine the olive oil, lemon juice, anchovy, garlic, and salt in a large salad bowl. Before serving, remove the garlic clove, then toss the fennel and green beans in the dressing. Sprinkle the olives and grind the pepper over the top. *Serves 4.*

TOMATO, AVOCADO, AND RED ONION SALAD

The lovely combination of the slightly acid tomatoes and the butter-smooth avocado is punctuated with the sweet bite of the red onion.

4 ripe tomatoes, cored
2 ripe avocados
Juice of 1 lemon
½ very small red onion,
*   peeled, sliced paper-thin*
*   and separated into rings*

Balsamic or red wine vinegar
*   to taste*
Fruity olive oil to taste
Freshly ground black pepper

Cut the tomatoes crosswise into ½-inch slices. Set aside. Cut the avocados in half lengthwise, remove the pits, and peel. Cut the avocado halves lengthwise into thin slices. Sprinkle lemon juice over the pieces to prevent discoloration.

Arrange the tomatoes so they just overlap along the bottom edge of individual salad plates or a platter. Place the avocado slices in a fan shape above the tomatoes. Sprinkle the onion rings on top of the tomato slices. Lightly sprinkle vinegar and oil to taste over the vegetables. Grind fresh black pepper over the whole salad. *Serves 4 to 6.*

ROASTED RED PEPPER SALAD WITH BASIL

We sampled a beautiful variation of this recipe at the City Cafe in Los Angeles: roasted and peeled red peppers cut into strips 1½ inches wide were layered on individual plates with whole fresh basil leaves and feta cheese, and then dressed with olive oil and lemon juice.

5 red bell peppers, roasted, peeled, and seeded (see page 94)
¼ cup olive oil
Juice of 1 lemon

Coarse salt and freshly ground pepper to taste
1 bunch fresh basil leaves, or 2 teaspoons dried basil leaves, crumbled

Slice the roasted peppers lengthwise into thin strips about ¼ inch wide, and place in a bowl. Dress with the olive oil, lemon juice, salt, and pepper. To cut the basil leaves, place leaves one on top of another, roll up like a cigar, and cut the roll into thin strips. Add the basil to the peppers, toss, and correct the seasoning. Marinate at room temperature for at least 1 hour before serving. *Serves 6 to 8.*

ORANGE AND FENNEL SALAD

A recipe from Palermo given to us by Viana's mother. The natural sweetness of the fennel and the oranges is brought into balance by the olive oil, salt, and freshly ground pepper. This light and incredibly refreshing salad, perfect after fish, can also be made with pink and yellow grapefruit instead of the oranges.

3 large navel oranges
2 medium fennel bulbs
3 tablespoons fruity olive oil

Coarse salt and freshly ground pepper to taste

Peel the oranges with a sharp knife, removing all the white pith. Slice crosswise into ¼-inch-thick rounds. Remove any seeds. Trim any bruised, discolored, or tough outer leaves from the fennel, trim the root end, and cut the bulb in half lengthwise. Cut out the core at the base of the fennel bulb. Cut the fennel lengthwise into julienne strips. Arrange the orange slices on a platter. Distribute the fennel over the oranges. Drizzle with the olive oil and season with the salt and pepper. Toss gently and serve. *Serves 4.*

WINTER SALAD

There is a tonic quality to these fresh, crisp, "rooty" vegetables—a restorative during winter. An unusual feature is the thinly sliced raw artichoke heart. Toss with the dressing just before serving.

2 medium leeks
2 artichokes
¼ cup lemon juice
1 large fennel bulb
1 celery heart, thinly sliced
    crosswise

10 radishes, peeled and cut
    into paper-thin rounds
3 carrots, peeled and cut into
    paper-thin rounds

DRESSING:

½ cup fruity olive oil
¼ cup lemon juice
2 teaspoons Dijon mustard

2 teaspoons coarse salt
Freshly ground pepper to taste

Make the dressing: Combine the olive oil, lemon juice, mustard, salt, and pepper in a small bowl. Set aside.

Trim the leeks, discarding all but the white part. Cut the leeks crosswise into thin rounds and rinse under cold running water. Drain. Remove all the leaves and the chokes from the artichokes so just the cleaned hearts remain. Dip the hearts into the lemon juice to prevent discoloration. Cut the hearts with a stainless steel knife into thin slices. Immediately immerse the slices in the prepared dressing. Trim any outer bruised, discolored, or tough leaves from the fennel bulb. Trim the root end and cut in half lengthwise. Cut out the core at the base of the bulb, and slice the bulb into slivers. Immediately before serving, toss all the vegetables in a salad bowl with just enough dressing to lightly coat; the salad will wilt if allowed to sit in the dressing. *Serves 4.*

CARROT SALAD WITH GORGONZOLA CREAM

Crunchy and creamy, salty and sweet, this pretty, delicate salad is best served as a separate course.

1½ pounds carrots, peeled and tops trimmed
3 large celery stalks, strings removed, and minced
4 ounces sweet gorgonzola cheese
1 tablespoon fruity olive oil

1 cup heavy cream
Coarse salt and freshly ground pepper to taste
Red cabbage, lettuce, or radicchio leaves for garnish

Grate the peeled carrots in a food processor or on the large hole of a four-sided grater. If the carrots are very wet after grating, roll them in paper towels to dry. Combine the grated carrots and minced celery in a bowl and set aside. Place half the gorgonzola in a small bowl. Mix in the olive oil with a fork. Add the heavy cream and mix until the cheese mixture is smooth. Add the remaining gorgonzola and stir so that it breaks up and adds texture to the dressing. Add salt and pepper. Pour the gorgonzola cream over the carrot and celery mixture. Toss to mix. Serve on individual plates on a bed of red cabbage, radicchio, or lettuce leaves. *Serves 6.*

DILLED CUCUMBER BEET SALAD

In Italy, beets are sold already roasted at produce stands. Slicing the beets and cucumbers paper-thin makes an elegant presentation with readily available vegetables. Try serving the salad as a beautiful plate garnish in place of a vegetable dish.

1 bunch beets, washed and
  tops trimmed, leaving 2
  inches
1 hot-house cucumber, peeled,
  or 2 cucumbers, peeled,
  halved, and seeded

1 cup yogurt
2 teaspoons minced fresh dill,
  or 1 teaspoon dried dill
Coarse salt to taste
Fresh dill sprigs for garnish

Place beets in shallow roasting pan and bake in a preheated 325° oven until tender, about 35 minutes. The time will vary depending on the freshness of the beets. Remove the beets from the oven and slip off the skins. Let cool. Slice the beets paper-thin using a mandoline or very sharp knife. Place in a bowl and set aside. Slice the cucumbers paper-thin using a mandoline or very sharp knife. Add the cucumbers to the beets. In small bowl, mix together the yogurt, dill, and salt. Pour the yogurt mixture over the beets and cucumbers and toss lightly to mix. Garnish with fresh dill sprigs. *Serves 4 to 6.*

ASPARAGUS AND CARROT JULIENNE

A real ode to spring, this salad is colorful, crisp, and sweet-tasting. The asparagus and carrots can be prepared in advance, wrapped in paper towels, and refrigerated until needed. Combine with the dressing just before serving.

1 pound thin asparagus, tough ends trimmed
1 pound tender carrots, peeled
3 tablespoons fruity olive oil
¼ cup lemon juice
Coarse salt and freshly ground pepper to taste

Cut the asparagus into 3-inch lengths. Cut the carrots into julienne pieces the same size as the asparagus. Cook the asparagus in an abundant amount of boiling salted water until tender but crisp, about 8 minutes. Drain and refresh under cold running water or in a bowl of ice water. Place the asparagus on paper towels to dry completely. Repeat the procedure with the carrots. Just before serving, combine the asparagus and carrots in a bowl with the olive oil and lemon juice. Toss gently, seasoning with salt and pepper. *Serves 4 to 6.*

WHITE BEAN, RED ONION, TOMATO, AND OREGANO SALAD

White beans with their mild flavor and creamy texture can be so good in bean salads. Known as cannellini in Italy, these beans are high in protein and inexpensive. We like this salad for the way the freshness of the tomato combines with the smooth texture of the bean and the sharp taste of the red onion and oregano.

2 cups cooked white beans, tender yet firm
¼ cup fruity olive oil
Coarse salt and freshly ground pepper to taste
2 large firm ripe tomatoes, peeled, seeded, and diced

¼ cup finely diced red onion
2 tablespoons fresh oregano leaves, cut into thin strips, or 2 teaspoons dried oregano leaves, crumbled

Drain the beans of any liquid and place them in a small bowl. Season them with the olive oil, salt, and pepper. Then toss with the tomatoes, red onion, and oregano. Taste for salt and pepper. *Serves 4.*

Tomato and Mozzarella

We present here three variations on a theme. The first is a classic combination of tomato, mozzarella, and basil; the second is a more robust version combining cherry tomatoes, mozzarella, oregano, and capers; the third is a winter rendition of sun-dried tomatoes and sliced mozzarella.

The simplicity of each of these dishes demands superior ingredients. You need tomatoes that *taste* and cheese that is not like a rubber ball. Mozzarella should have a fresh, light flavor with a moist yet firm texture. For our purposes, fresh domestic mozzarella in water is the best choice. The highly perishable nature of the true Italian mozzarella made from buffalo milk makes it almost impossible for the imported cheese to survive the journey. Even though it is becoming more available in specialty shops, it is best to avoid it, unfortunately, in favor of the fresh domestic product. If domestic mozzarella in water is hard to come by, an adequate substitute is whole-milk mozzarella.

CAPRESE
tomato and mozzarella slices with basil

It is important to cut the tomato slices thick enough to stand up to the cheese. The mild flavor of the mozzarella can stand a good bit of the acid crunch it gets from the tomato. The excitement of this dish is the juxtaposition of the sweet bite of the tomato and the mild freshness of the cheese.

CONTINUED

4 ripe firm tomatoes
1 pound mozzarella
Red wine vinegar (optional)

4–5 medium fresh basil leaves
Fruity olive oil

Wash, core, and cut the tomatoes into slices slightly thicker than ¼ inch. Slice the mozzarella a little thinner than the tomato slices, but being careful not to make them too thin. Taste the tomatoes. If they lack a citrus-acid bite, sprinkle a little vinegar on them. Cut the basil into julienne strips by placing one leaf atop another. Roll up the stack and cut into thin slices. Arrange the tomatoes and mozzarella slices alternately on a serving plate. Sprinkle the basil over the tomatoes and cheese. Drizzle the oil over all. Serve immediately. *Serves 4 to 6.*

TOMATO AND MOZZARELLA WITH CAPERS AND OREGANO

This salad should have a strong oregano flavor. To intensify the herbal flavor use oregano-flavored oil. This dish is a nice alternative to the more familiar tomato, mozzarella, and basil salad.

2 baskets cherry tomatoes
¼ cup fruity olive oil, or
  oregano-flavored oil
1 pound mozzarella, cut into
  ½-inch dice

2 tablespoons giant capers
2–3 tablespoons fresh oregano
  leaves, cut into thin
  slivers, or 3 teaspoons
  dried oregano leaves
Coarse salt

Cut the cherry tomatoes in half. Place the olive oil in a salad bowl or deep platter, add the tomatoes, mozzarella, capers, and oregano and toss to lightly coat. Salt generously. Set the mixture aside for a few minutes to blend the flavors. Serve with good bread to soak up all the juices. *Serves 6 to 8.*

SUN-DRIED TOMATOES AND MOZZARELLA ANTIPASTO

Try this dish when good fresh tomatoes are out of season. The sweetness of the sun-dried tomatoes needs the bite of vinegar as a balance. Fresh parsley is available all year round.

½ cup fruity olive oil
½ teaspoon red pepper flakes
1 pound mozzarella
Coarse salt to taste
½ cup sun-dried tomatoes (see page 276)

2 tablespoons red wine vinegar
¼ cup pitted oil-cured black olives, cut in half
1 tablespoon coarsely chopped fresh parsley leaves
Freshly ground pepper to taste

Combine the olive oil and red pepper flakes in a small cup and let sit 2 hours or longer. Cut the mozzarella into slices about ⅛ inch thick. Arrange the slices on a platter. Salt to taste. If you are using sun-dried cherry tomatoes, leave them whole; or if using large sun-dried tomatoes, cut into thick slivers. Toss the tomatoes with the vinegar in a bowl. Scatter the sun-dried tomatoes and olives over the cheese. Strain the red pepper flakes from the olive oil. Pour enough oil over the cheese, tomatoes, and olives to lightly coat. Sprinkle parsley and grind pepper on top. *Serves 4 to 6.*

INSALATA RUSSA
russian salad

The creamy, pale yellow mayonnaise combined with the color and crunch of the diced vegetables is delicious as well as lovely to behold. We use just enough mayonnaise to bind the vegetables. Anchovies add tang but are otherwise unobtrusive. Leave them out if they do not appeal to you. For an elegant presentation, surround the salad with radicchio leaves and garnish with thin slices of lemon. A wonderful buffet dish that can be made up to two days in advance.

*½ pound tender green beans,
    trimmed*
Coarse salt
3 medium carrots, peeled
3 medium boiling potatoes
*2 tablespoons finely chopped
    cornichons, or other good
    quality pickle in brine*
3 tablespoons capers

3 tablespoons olive oil
1 tablespoon red wine vinegar
*1 recipe Lemon Mayonnaise
    (see page 265)*
*3 canned flat anchovies, finely
    minced (optional)*
*Radicchio leaves and thin
    lemon slices for garnish
    (optional)*

Blanch the green beans in an abundant amount of boiling salted water until tender but crisp and bright green in color, about 10 minutes. Cooking time will vary according to age and variety of green beans. Drain. Refresh under cold running water and drain in a colander. Dry on paper towels.

Cook the carrots in an abundant amount of boiling salted water until tender but firm, about 15 minutes. Drain and dry on paper towels. Cover the potatoes with water by 2 inches in large saucepan. Boil until tender but not mushy, about 15 minutes. Drain and peel when cool enough to handle.

Cut the green beans, carrots, and potatoes into a very small dice. Combine with the cornichons and capers in a large bowl. Season with the olive oil, vinegar, and salt. Toss to mix. Add the mayonnaise and optional anchovies and mix thoroughly. Correct the seasonings. To serve, mound on a platter, and smooth the tops and sides. Garnish with radicchio leaves and lemon slices, if desired, or according to personal whim. *Serves 6.*

INSALATA COMPOSTA

composed salad

In Florence food is often served at room temperature, and at Coco Lezzone, a favorite restaurant of ours featuring traditional Tuscan food, almost everything is served at a temperature that falls somewhere between hot and cold. As we experienced it in Florence, Insalata

Composta is a sublime vegetable dish. Each vegetable in this salad is cooked and cooled separately, and in restaurants and trattorie the vegetables are arranged on a platter for display. The salad can be made with other seasonal vegetables such as Swiss chard, spinach, or fresh shelled beans. Just remember to keep the elements separate or the clarity of the dish is lost. At the table each person uses the lemon to season the vegetables to taste.

*2 or 3 large all-purpose
    potatoes*
*½ pound whole baby zucchini,
    or the smallest available,
    trimmed*
*½ pound tender green beans,
    trimmed*

*3 or 4 tablespoons fruity olive
    oil*
*Coarse salt and freshly ground
    pepper to taste*
Lemon wedges

Cook the potatoes in boiling salted water to cover in a medium saucepan until firm but tender, about 15 minutes. Drain. When cool enough to handle, peel and cut the potatoes into a medium dice. Cook the zucchini very briefly in boiling salted water until tender but very crisp, about 2 to 3 minutes. Drain and refresh under cold running water. Dry completely on paper towels. Cook the beans in boiling salted water until tender but crisp, about 5 to 10 minutes. Cooking time varies widely according to size. Drain and refresh under cold running water. Dry on paper towels.

Arrange the zucchini, green beans, and potatoes in separate rows on a platter. Drizzle the vegetables with the olive oil. Season with the salt and pepper. Toss lightly, keeping the rows separate. Taste and adjust seasonings. Garnish with lemon wedges. *Serves 4.*

INSALATA SPAGNOLA

spanish salad

This rich, lusty Spanish-inspired version of Insalata Russa (see page 66) is the most delicious potato salad known to man. Add green beans or beets, if desired. To serve as a main dish, accompany with skinless poached chicken lightly masked with aïoli.

4 small new potatoes
Coarse salt
1 medium artichoke heart, in acidulated water (see page 139)
2 medium carrots, peeled and cut into small dice

½ cup peas, fresh or frozen
½ cup fresh young fava beans
Freshly ground pepper to taste
1–2 cups Aïoli (see page 267), depending on taste

Boil the potatoes in salted water to cover in a large saucepan until tender, about 15 minutes. Drain. When cool enough to handle, peel and cut into a small dice. Drain the artichoke heart. Boil in salted water to cover in a saucepan until tender when pierced with the tip of a knife, about 10 minutes. Let cool and cut into a small dice. Cook the carrots briefly in boiling salted water to cover in a saucepan until tender but crisp, about 2 minutes. Drain and refresh under cold running water. Cook the frozen peas briefly in boiling salted water in a saucepan. If fresh, cook longer until tender. Time will vary depending on size and tenderness. Drain and refresh under cold running water. Cook the fava beans briefly in a little boiling salted water in a saucepan until bright green, about 5 minutes. Drain and refresh under cold running water. Combine all the vegetables in a large bowl. Season with salt and pepper. Gently fold in the aïoli. Correct the seasonings. Cover and chill until needed. *Serves 4.*

MEDITERRANEAN POTATO SALAD

This chunky potato and tomato salad is enlivened by the piquant presence of capers and green olives. As lettuces are not easily cultivated around the Mediterranean, vegetable salads are often served.

1½ pounds boiling potatoes, all about the same size
Coarse salt
2 medium firm ripe tomatoes
½ small red onion, peeled
¼ cup pitted green olives, coarsely chopped
1 tablespoon capers

1 small garlic clove, peeled and minced fine
¼ cup fruity olive oil
¼ cup imported good quality white wine vinegar
Salt and freshly ground pepper to taste

Cook the potatoes in boiling salted water in a medium pot until tender but firm, about 15 minutes. Cooking time will vary according to the size of the potatoes. Drain. Return the potatoes to the pot and toss over high heat to evaporate any remaining moisture. Set aside to cool. When cool enough to handle, peel with a paring knife, removing any bruised or discolored areas. Cut into roughly 1-inch dice, keeping them irregular in size. Core the tomatoes and cut into chunks about the same size as the potatoes. Cut the red onion into slices about ⅛ inch thick. Combine the potatoes, tomatoes, red onion, olives, capers, and garlic in a large bowl. Add the olive oil, vinegar, salt, and pepper. Toss gently to mix. Adjust the seasonings and serve. *Serves 4.*

CHICKEN AND ESCAROLE SALAD

The suavity of the chicken contrasts well with the punch of raw garlic and black pepper. The garlic-rubbed croutons add a crisp note and permeate the salad with their flavor. Take care not to overcook the chicken.

2 whole chicken breasts
Coarse salt and freshly ground
    pepper to taste
1 large head escarole
4 thick slices (1 inch) French
    or Italian bread

2 garlic cloves, peeled
½ cup olive oil
¼ cup red wine vinegar

Season the chicken breasts with salt and pepper. Roast in a preheated 450° oven for 12 to 15 minutes or until the juices run clear and the meat is no longer pink near the bone. When cool enough to handle, remove the skin and bones and shred the chicken into bite-size strips. Remove the tough outer leaves of the escarole and wash the remaining leaves thoroughly. Dry well and tear into bite-size pieces. To make the croutons, cut the bread into 1-inch dice. Place in a preheated 250° oven for 12 minutes or until crisped. Lightly rub the croutons with the raw garlic. Toss together the chicken, escarole, and croutons in a salad bowl with the olive oil and vinegar, adding salt and pepper to taste. *Serves 4 to 6.*

pasta and rice salads

PASTA SALADS

PENNE ALLA CAPRESE
penne with tomato, mozzarella, and basil

A classic combination of flavors of which we never tire. This is our standard pasta salad during summer months when tomatoes are bursting with flavor and basil is fragrant and abundant. In Italy it is common to combine a room-temperature uncooked sauce with hot pasta during summer months.

4 large tomatoes, peeled and
  cut into ½-inch dice
2–3 tablespoons fresh basil
  leaves, chopped, or 2
  teaspoons dried basil
  leaves, crumbled
2 garlic cloves, peeled and
  minced

Coarse salt and freshly ground
  pepper to taste
Fruity olive oil to cover
1 pound penne rigate or
  rigatoni
¾ pound mozzarella, grated
  on large hole side of
  grater

Mix together the tomatoes, basil, garlic, salt, and pepper in a small
bowl. Add enough olive oil to just cover the tomatoes. Let marinate
at room temperature or in the refrigerator for at least 2 hours so
that flavors mix and juices form. Just before serving, cook penne in
abundant, salted, boiling water about 15 minutes or until al dente.
Drain pasta, place in serving bowl, and immediately add tomato
mixture, which has been brought to room temperature if refrigerated,
and grated mozzarella. Toss pasta so that mozzarella begins to melt.
Serve immediately. *Serves 4.*

INSALATA DI PASTA DEL GIARDINO

*pasta salad with raw
garden vegetables*

The recent mania for small, immature vegetables may sometimes
seem to be an annoying affectation, but zucchini in its infant stage
is truly a very special vegetable. The hot pasta in this salad lightly

cooks the baby zucchini and tomato, takes the raw edge off the celery and carrots, and releases the fragrance of the basil. Baby zucchini are only a few inches long with a delicacy of flavor and texture unmatched by the more mature vegetable. If unavailable, look for the smallest, firmest zucchini you can find.

1 pound rigatoni
½ pound baby zucchini, or the smallest available, trimmed and cut into small dice
½ medium red onion, peeled and cut into small dice
½ medium hot-house cucumber, peeled, seeded, and cut into small dice
2 celery stalks, strings removed, cut into small dice

2 large tomatoes, peeled, seeded, and cut into small dice
2 carrots, peeled and minced
½ cup chopped fresh basil leaves
½ cup fruity olive oil
Coarse salt and freshly ground pepper to taste
Cruet of fruity olive oil
Pepper mill

Cook the pasta as directed on the package. Combine the vegetables and chopped basil in a large serving bowl. Drain the pasta well. Add the hot pasta and olive oil to the vegetables. Season with salt and pepper. Toss well to mix. Serve with the cruet of olive oil and pepper mill on the table. *Serves 4.*

PASTA SALAD WITH CHICKEN AND VEGETABLES

This hearty main-course pasta salad is full of satisfying flavors and textures. We enjoy the flavor that roasting gives the chicken, but be careful not to overcook it. Serve the pasta salad with grissini (bread sticks), and follow with fruit.

DRESSING:

1 tablespoon minced fresh rosemary leaves, or 1 teaspoon dried rosemary leaves, crumbled
½ cup olive oil
3 teaspoons red wine vinegar

1 teaspoon Dijon mustard
Coarse salt and freshly ground pepper to taste

1 large whole chicken breast
Coarse salt and freshly ground pepper to taste
2 sprigs fresh rosemary, or 2 teaspoons dried rosemary leaves, crumbled
2 zucchini, ends trimmed
2 carrots, peeled
2 celery stalks, strings removed

1 red bell pepper, halved and seeded
¼ pound tender green beans, trimmed
½ pound penne
1 teaspoon capers
Sprigs fresh rosemary for garnish (optional)

To make the dressing, heat the rosemary in the olive oil in a small saucepan until the oil is hot, but not smoking. Cool for 30 minutes. If you are using dried rosemary, strain. Combine the oil with the vinegar, mustard, salt, and pepper in a small bowl. Set aside.

Meanwhile, rub the chicken breast generously with the salt, pepper, and rosemary. Roast in a preheated 450° oven for 10 to 12 minutes or until the juices run clear and the meat is no longer pink near the bone. Cool. Cut the zucchini, carrots, celery, and red pepper in julienne strips. Cut any long green beans into pieces about as long as the vegetables. Blanch each vegetable in an abundant amount of boiling salted water until tender. Remove each vegetable with a slotted spoon and place in colander. Refresh under cold running water. Cut the cooled chicken into julienne strips. Cook the penne as directed on the package. Drain. Toss the pasta gently with the chicken, vegetables, and dressing in a large bowl. Scatter the capers over the top. If using fresh rosemary, garnish with rosemary sprigs. This salad can be made up to 1 day ahead. *Serves 4 to 6.*

CAPELLINI WITH SUN-DRIED TOMATO "PESTO"

This light and spicy pasta salad serves approximately 10 people as part of a buffet, or 6 to 8 as a first course. Leftover salad can be used in the recipe for Pasta Frittata (see page 107). Another option is to make individual frittatas, using 2 eggs and ½ cup capellini salad per frittata.

1 cup olive oil from sun-dried tomatoes (if you don't have enough flavored oil, add olive oil to equal 1 cup)

1 cup sun-dried tomatoes, cut into thin strips
1½ teaspoons cayenne pepper or to taste
1 pound capellini

Combine ¼ cup of the olive oil, ½ cup of the sun-dried tomatoes, and the cayenne in a food processor. Process until the tomatoes become a rough paste. Combine this paste with the remaining olive oil in a bowl. Cook the capellini according to the directions on the package. Drain. Gently toss the capellini in a large bowl with the olive oil and tomato paste mixture. Scatter the remaining sun-dried tomato strips over the salad. Let the salad stand for several hours. Serve cold or at room temperature. *Serves 6 to 8 as a first course.*

PENNE WITH SHRIMP, TOMATO, AND MINT

Ordinarily we are not enamored of bay shrimp, but they work well in this dish, giving almost every bite a sweet taste of shrimp. Larger shrimp may also be used.

1 pound cooked bay shrimp
5 tablespoons olive oil
1 pound penne
1 can (28 ounces) peeled
   Italian tomatoes, or 8
   large tomatoes, peeled
   and seeded

1 cup fresh mint leaves,
   minced, or 1 tablespoon
   dried mint leaves,
   crumbled
Coarse salt and freshly ground
   pepper to taste

Sauté the shrimp in 2 tablespoons of oil in a skillet until pink. Set aside. Cook the penne according to the package directions. Drain.

To make the sauce, purée the canned or fresh tomatoes with their juice in a food processor or blender. Heat the remaining olive oil in a medium skillet. Add the tomato purée and cook over medium heat, stirring occasionally, for 10 minutes. Add the shrimp, mint, salt, and pepper and continue cooking until the sauce reduces slightly, about 5 minutes. Let sauce cool. Toss with the pasta in a large bowl. *Serves 4 to 6.*

COUNTRY-STYLE RIGATONI SALAD

This satisfying vegetable pasta salad features the fresh, strong flavor of broccoli. The stalks as well as the flowerets are used. The sweet and meaty stalks, when peeled, are very tender. Look for broccoli with a deep green or purplish color. If yellowed or starting to flower, it's past its prime.

PESTO DRESSING:

1 cup fresh basil leaves

3 garlic cloves, peeled and minced

4 tablespoons grated Parmesan cheese

2 teaspoons pine nuts

½ cup olive oil

Coarse salt to taste

Combine all the ingredients except the salt in a blender or food processor. Process until blended but with a somewhat coarse texture. Add salt. Set aside.

PASTA SALAD:

2 pounds broccoli

2 long strips lemon peel

Coarse salt to taste

1 pound rigatoni

1 pound mushrooms, rinsed and wiped clean with paper towels

3 tablespoons olive oil

Freshly ground pepper to taste

6 medium tomatoes, cored and cut into sections

2 bunches green onions, trimmed and cut into thin rounds

Separate the broccoli flowerets from the stalks, and break the flowerets into large bite-size pieces. Peel the stalks with a paring knife. Cut into rough julienne strips. Place the lemon peel in a large pot containing an abundant amount of water. Bring to a boil. Add salt. Add the broccoli pieces and cook until tender but still crisp, about 5 minutes. Remove the broccoli with a slotted spoon and place in a colander. Refresh under cold running water to set the color and stop further cooking.

Add the rigatoni to the boiling water. Cook until tender. Drain in a colander. Run cold water over the pasta and drain again. Reserve the lemon peel. While the rigatoni is cooking, trim mushroom stems. Cut in half or, if very large, in quarters. Sauté in 3 tablespoons olive oil over very high heat for 2 to 3 minutes. Season with salt and pepper.

Gently toss the rigatoni with the lemon peel, pesto, broccoli, mushrooms, tomatoes, and green onions in a large bowl. Add salt and pepper. Remove the lemon peel. Adjust the seasonings and serve. *Serves 6.*

SPAGHETTINI SALAD WITH SPICY SCALLOPS

The juices of the scallops are absorbed by the spaghettini, permeating the pasta itself with the flavor of the scallops.

2 dried red chile peppers, or
    to taste
1 pound scallops, muscle
    removed and cut in half if
    large
½ cup fruity olive oil
4 large garlic cloves, peeled
    and lightly crushed

½ cup chopped fresh flat-leaf
    parsley
Juice of 2 lemons
2 teaspoons coarse salt
Freshly ground pepper
½ pound spaghettini

Sauté the chile peppers and scallops in half the oil in a skillet over high heat until the scallops are just opaque. Remove from the heat; the scallops will continue to cook as they cool. Combine the scallops, remaining olive oil, and garlic cloves in a bowl and refrigerate. When cool, add the chopped parsley, lemon juice, salt, and pepper. Marinate in the refrigerator for 1 to 3 hours. Cook the spaghettini according to the package directions. Drain. Before serving, remove the garlic cloves from the scallop mixture and toss the scallops with the spaghettini. Let the mixture stand in the refrigerator for about 1 hour or until all the liquid is absorbed. *Serves 4 as a first course.*

GNOCCHETTI RIGATI ALLA MENTA

This brilliantly colored pasta salad has a fresh, immediate flavor heightened by the cool taste and fragrant perfume of mint. Select very ripe red tomatoes and deep red bell peppers to get the proper intensity of color. Although this is not technically a cold pasta dish, part of its beauty is the contrast of the hot pasta and cool sauce.

4 large tomatoes, peeled and seeded

4 large meaty red bell peppers, roasted, peeled, and seeded (see page 94)

10 large whole fresh mint leaves

2 garlic cloves, peeled and minced

¼ cup fruity olive oil

Coarse salt and freshly ground pepper to taste

1 pound gnocchetti rigati

1–2 tablespoons olive oil for pasta

Fresh mint leaves for garnish

Place the tomatoes in a food processor. Chop to a fine, coarse texture, stopping short of a smooth purée. Place peppers along with any collected juice in a food processor. Chop to a fine, coarse texture as with the tomatoes. Combine the tomatoes and peppers in a small bowl. Add the mint leaves, garlic, olive oil, salt, and pepper. Stir well. Cover and refrigerate for several hours. Bring to room temperature. Cook the pasta according to the directions on the package. Drain well. Toss the hot pasta and a little olive oil in a large bowl. Add the tomato-pepper mixture and toss well. Garnish with mint leaves and grind additional pepper over the top. *Serves 4 to 6.*

RIGATONI WITH PEPERONATA

In Italy, peperonata is traditionally served as an accompaniment to eggs and simply prepared meats. The piquant, sweet flavor of the pepper-tomato mixture is absorbed by the rigatoni in this salad. Rigatoni is particularly sturdy and has great texture when cooked al dente.

1 pound rigatoni
4 garlic cloves, peeled and
*   minced*
1 large red onion, peeled and
*   coarsely chopped*
¼ cup olive oil
4 red bell peppers, halved,
*   seeded and cut lengthwise*
*   into ½-inch strips*

¼ cup red wine vinegar
6 small tomatoes, peeled,
*   seeded, and coarsely*
*   chopped*
Coarse salt to taste

Cook the pasta by boiling in an abundant amount of boiling salted water in a large pot for about 12 minutes or until al dente. Drain the rigatoni in a colander and run under cold water until it feels cool to the touch. Let drain. Set aside.

To prepare the peperonata, sauté the garlic and onion in the oil in a large skillet. When the garlic begins to give off its odor, add the peppers. Sauté gently, stirring frequently, until the peppers are limp. Add the vinegar and cook, covered, for 3 minutes. Add the tomatoes and cook, uncovered, until the tomatoes give off their juice and the juices thicken. Taste for salt. Let mixture cool to room temperature. Combine with the rigatoni in a bowl. This dish can be refrigerated for 2 days. Bring back to room temperature before serving so that the olive oil liquifies. *Serves 4 to 6.*

PASTA ALL'ERBE
pasta shells with herbs

This pasta salad is perfect eating during the summer when the garden yields forth a profusion of pungent herbs. Use whatever herbs are freshest and most available to you, such as basil, rosemary, oregano, parsley, thyme, or sage. This dish is fun to prepare tableside: Place the herbs in a rustic serving bowl, and as you pour the warm oil over them a pungent, herbal fragrance will delight your guests.

1 pound pasta shells
1 or 2 dried hot red peppers to taste

1 cup fresh herbs, stems removed, coarsely chopped
5 tablespoons fruity olive oil

Cook the pasta according to package directions, adding the dried hot pepper to the pasta cooking water. Drain the pasta, discarding the hot pepper. Place the herbs in a serving bowl. Heat the olive oil in a small saucepan until very warm but not smoking, and pour over the herbs. Toss the pasta in the bowl with the herb-oil mixture. Serve immediately. *Serves 4.*

RICE SALADS

CELEBRATION RICE

We created this dish for a dear friend's wedding. We wanted the food to reflect the joy of the occasion and thus color was paramount. If you are blessed with a large supply of saffron, use it. It is impossible to use too much in this recipe.

2 quarts chicken broth or
   water
1–2 teaspoons saffron threads
1 teaspoon turmeric
1 tablespoon coarse salt
2 cups long-grain white rice
1 onion, peeled and finely
   chopped

Vinaigrette (see Wild and
   White Rice Salad,
   Dressing, page 88)
1 teaspoon rosewater
   (optional)
3 tablespoons pomegranate
   seeds for garnish

Fill a large pot with 2 quarts chicken broth or hot water. Add the saffron and turmeric and let sit until spices color the water, about 5 minutes. Add the salt to the water and bring to a boil over high heat. Add the rice and onion and cook until the rice is tender yet still firm to the bite. Do not overcook! Drain the rice through a fine sieve. Run cold water over the rice until it feels cool to the touch. Some of the yellow color will drain away but the rice will nevertheless retain a bright color. Shake to drain water. When the rice is fairly dry, place in a large bowl. Add the vinaigrette, and, if desired, the rosewater. Toss the rice to mix and place in a serving bowl. Scatter the pomegranate seeds on top for decoration. *Serves 10.*

RISO PRIMAVERA
spring rice salad

A colorful salad which lends itself to improvisation. Other tender seasonal vegetables can be added as well as cooked meats and fish.

1 pound long-grain white rice

4 ripe tomatoes, cored, halved lengthwise, seeded, and cut lengthwise into ¼-inch-thick strips

3 small bell peppers of assorted colors (red, yellow, green), halved, seeded, and cut lengthwise into ¼-inch-thick strips

2 celery stalks, peeled and cut into small dice

6 small tender carrots, peeled and cut into thin rounds

10 fresh basil leaves, or 2 teaspoons dried basil leaves, crumbled

¼ cup fruity olive oil

Juice of 2 lemons

Coarse salt and freshly ground pepper to taste

Cook the rice in an abundant amount of boiling salted water in a large pot until the grains are tender yet still firm to the bite. Drain the rice in a fine sieve. Run cold water over the rice until it feels cool to the touch. Drain the rice thoroughly. Combine the tomatoes, peppers, celery, and carrots in medium bowl. Cut the fresh basil into julienne strips by placing one leaf atop another, rolling up the stack, and cutting crosswise into thin slices. Toss the basil to separate the thin strands. Add to the bowl of vegetables along with the olive oil, lemon juice, salt, and pepper. Toss to mix. Add the drained rice and toss thoroughly. *Serves 6 to 8 as a side dish.*

WILD AND WHITE RICE SALAD

This basic salad can be made with all white rice. Basmati, an unprocessed white rice imported from India, is particularly flavorful and nutritious. This recipe can be used as a base for a luncheon dish simply by adding 1 or 2 cups of cooked meat or fish and/or any cooked vegetables you may have on hand.

1 cup long-grain white rice
1 cup wild rice
½ small red onion, peeled and minced

3 celery stalks, peeled and minced
¼ cup minced fresh parsley

DRESSING:

½ cup vegetable oil
2 tablespoons olive oil
4 tablespoons balsamic vinegar, or ¼ cup red wine vinegar

2–3 teaspoons Dijon mustard
Coarse salt and freshly ground pepper to taste

Cook the rices separately in abundant amounts of boiling salted water until the grains are tender yet still firm to the bite. If using basmati, rinse the rice in several changes of water before cooking. Cook the white rice for about 7 to 10 minutes, and the wild rice for about 30 to 40 minutes. Drain the cooked rice in a large sieve and run cold water over the grains until they feel cool to the touch. Drain the rice thoroughly. Mix with the onion, celery, and parsley in a large bowl. Combine the dressing ingredients in a small bowl. Pour over the rice mixture. Toss thoroughly to mix. Add salt and pepper to taste. Rice salad will generally keep for up to 3 to 4 days, covered, in the refrigerator. *Serves 6 to 8.*

INSALATA DI RISO SELVATICO
wild rice salad

The grain known as wild rice is in fact a cereal still collected by hand by Indians in the Lake Superior area. The dark-colored grain has a special, woodsy flavor which complements game and fowl.

2 boxes (4 ounces) wild rice
¼ cup pine nuts
8–10 sun-dried tomatoes, halved (optional, see page 276)
½ cup black oil-cured olives, pitted
1 tablespoon minced fresh parsley leaves
½ cup olive oil
¼ cup red wine vinegar
Coarse salt and freshly ground pepper to taste

Cook the wild rice in an abundant amount of boiling salted water in a large pot for 35 to 45 minutes or until the grains have almost doubled in size and are tender, but still chewy. Drain the rice in a sieve and run cold water over to cool. Drain thoroughly. Toast the pine nuts lightly in a skillet over low heat until golden brown. Let cool. Combine the drained wild rice in a bowl with the pine nuts, sun-dried tomatoes, olives, parsley, olive oil, vinegar, salt, and pepper. Toss gently to mix. *Serves 4 to 6.*

cheese and eggs

MASCARPONE

Mascarpone is an Italian fresh cheese similar to our cream cheese. There are some key differences, however: mascarpone is at once more dense than cream cheese in texture and lighter on the tongue. There is also a natural sweetness to the cheese. Traditionally used on breads for breakfast and in desserts, we highly recommend that you find a source for this unique cheese. Lacking that, the following recipe is a good substitute to use in the dessert recipes which call for fresh mascarpone (see pages 253 and 254).

¾ *pound cream cheese*   *Juice of ½ lemon*
¼ *pound ricotta cheese*   *1 tablespoon sugar*
2 tablespoons heavy cream

In an electric mixer or food processor, mix together all the ingredients until smooth and creamy. Refrigerate, covered, until ready to use. It will last up to one week. *Makes about 1 pound.*

HOMEMADE RICOTTA

This ricotta must be served just as it cools to really enjoy the farm-fresh dairy flavor, aroma, and light, moist texture. Refrigeration destroys the delicacy of the homemade cheese. Serve with green olives, lemon wedges, and good bread.

2 quarts whole milk   *Coarse salt and freshly ground*
1 cup heavy cream   *pepper to taste*
2–4 tablespoons lemon juice   *Fruity olive oil*

Bring the milk and cream to a simmer very slowly in a saucepan. Turn off heat. Add the lemon juice a little at a time and stir. Use only enough lemon juice needed to curdle the milk and cream. The mixture should separate into curds and whey in a matter of seconds. When the mixture curdles, pour into a colander lined with a double thickness of dampened cheesecloth. Allow to drain at least 1 hour or until very thick. Place the drained ricotta on a serving platter. As soon as it has cooled, sprinkle with a generous amount of salt and a grind of black pepper. Drizzle with olive oil. *Makes 2 cups. Serves 4 to 6 as a first course.*

RICOTTA WITH HERBS

Delicious as a light and tasty alternative to cottage cheese. Served with crostini (see page 9), Ricotta with Herbs makes an inexpensive spread for hors d'oeuvre; or, combine with prosciutto in a sandwich.

2 green onions, trimmed of all but 2 inches of green, or 2 tablespoons snipped fresh chives
1 pound ricotta
1 tablespoon finely chopped parsley leaves

3 fresh basil leaves, chopped
Juice of ½ lemon
1 tablespoon fruity olive oil
Coarse salt and freshly ground pepper to taste

Cut the green onions in half lengthwise, then chop fine. Place the ricotta in a bowl and beat with a wire whisk until smooth and creamy. Add the herbs, green onion, lemon juice, olive oil, salt, and pepper. Mix well. Cover and place in refrigerator at least 30 minutes for flavors to blend. *Serves 8 to 10 as an appetizer.*

ROASTED RED PEPPERS STUFFED WITH RICOTTA

These peppers require patience and careful handling. Choosing heavy, meaty peppers will make them easier to work with and less likely to tear once they are peeled. The dramatic results are well worth the extra time required. These bright, shiny red peppers, topped with a jaunty basil leaf, are dear to our hearts and make an especially charming first course or luncheon dish.

4 large smooth red bell
peppers
Coarse salt and freshly ground
pepper to taste

4 cups ricotta
¼ cup fruity olive oil
Juice of 1 lemon
4 large basil sprigs

Roast the peppers over a gas flame or under a broiler, using tongs to turn the peppers until they are completely blackened. Place them immediately into a plastic bag. Close the bag and let the peppers sweat for 10 minutes. Peel the peppers carefully under cold running water so as not to tear them. Place the peppers on paper towels to dry. Cut a slit in the bottom of each pepper and carefully remove the seeds and membranes, trying to keep the peppers whole. Add salt and pepper to the ricotta in a bowl and mix. Spoon the ricotta into a pastry bag fitted with a large plain tube. Pipe the ricotta into each pepper from the bottom opening until the pepper assumes its former shape. Combine the olive oil and lemon juice with salt to taste in a small bowl. Place the peppers on a plate and lightly coat with the dressing. The dressing should pool on the plate. Insert the basil sprig next to the stem. *Serves 4.*

RICOTTA AL FORNO
baked ricotta with black olives

Baked ricotta is rustic looking with a golden, crusty exterior, and it has a direct, uncomplicated flavor. As it cools it will lose some volume, becoming dense and compact. Baked ricotta is moist and delicious and perfect on a picnic with bread and a simple robust red wine. Cut into wedges and serve. Some brands of commercially made ricotta contain gelatin which gives the cheese a firmer texture and eliminates the need to drain the cheese first. Variations include the addition of fresh thyme and prosciutto to the cheese.

2 containers (15 ounces each) ricotta, or 2 pounds fresh ricotta
2 tablespoons butter
¼ cup bread crumbs
4 eggs

½ cup grated Parmesan cheese
¾ cup pitted black olives, quartered
Coarse salt and freshly ground pepper to taste

If the ricotta is watery, drain by placing it in a large square of double-thickness cheesecloth. Gather together two diagonally opposite ends of the cheesecloth and tie, forming a ball. Tie the other two ends around the faucet over the kitchen sink. Allow to drain at least 1 hour.

Butter an 8-inch springform pan or a soufflé dish at least 3 inches deep. Coat with bread crumbs and shake off excess crumbs. Combine the ricotta, eggs, and Parmesan in a medium bowl and mix with a spoon until blended. Stir in the olives. Season cautiously with salt and pepper to taste, remembering that the olives are salty. Pour the mixture into the prepared springform or soufflé dish. Bake in preheated 375° oven for 1 hour and 15 minutes or until the top is firm and golden. Let cool. Unmold onto a serving plate. The finished baked ricotta deflates a little as it cools. Slice into wedges. Serve with bread drizzled with herb-flavored olive oil. *Serves 4 to 6.*

RICOTTA SALATA AND AVOCADO IN CHILE PEPPER OIL

Look for the Haas variety of avocado: It has a dark, almost black, rough-textured skin and a very rich flavor. Occasionally a Fuerte avocado at the proper stage of ripeness tastes as good as a Haas. The gigantic Florida avocados are watery and flavorless. A ripe avocado should yield to gentle pressure. Red chile pepper oil, available in Chinese food stores and in the Asian section of supermarkets, can be substituted for the dried pepper and olive oil.

1 teaspoon crushed dried red chile peppers
½ cup fruity olive oil
1 pound ricotta salata (see p. 99) or feta cheese, cut into ¼-inch-thick slices

Freshly ground pepper to taste
2 avocados, large and meaty
2 lemons
1 cup oil-cured olives

Combine the crushed chile peppers with the olive oil in a small bowl and let marinate for 1 hour or longer. Arrange the ricotta salata slices on a platter. Pour the spicy olive oil over the cheese and grind a little black pepper over all. Cut the avocados in half lengthwise and remove the pits. Make 3 cuts along the length of the skin, cutting in only as deep as the skin. Peel off the skin. Cut the avocado halves lengthwise into slices about ½ inch thick. Arrange the avocado slices on the platter. Sprinkle the avocado with the juice of 1 lemon. Arrange the olives in the center of platter. Cut the remaining lemon in wedges and remove seeds. Garnish platter with lemon wedges and serve immediately. *Serves 4 to 6.*

MARINATED GOAT CHEESE WITH SUN-DRIED TOMATOES

The sweet flavor and chewy texture of the sun-dried tomatoes are a perfect contrast to the tart, lemony goat cheese. Drizzle a little of the herb-flavored oil on a slice of peasant bread, spread with some goat cheese, and eat with the sun-dried tomatoes.

1–2 cups fruity olive oil, enough to completely cover cheese

10 black peppercorns

2 sprigs fresh rosemary, or 1 teaspoon dried rosemary leaves, crumbled

2 sprigs fresh sage, or 1 teaspoon dried sage leaves, crumbled

2 sprigs fresh thyme, or 1 teaspoon dried thyme leaves, crumbled

3–4 whole garlic cloves, peeled

½ cup sun-dried tomatoes (see page 276)

2 small goat cheeses

Combine ¼ cup of the oil, the peppercorns, herbs, and garlic in a small saucepan. Heat until warm. Let cool. Arrange a few of the sun-dried tomatoes on the bottom of a mason jar or similar wide-mouth container that is a little larger than the cheeses. Place the goat cheeses in jar and arrange the remaining sun-dried tomatoes around them. Pour the cooled olive oil with herbs, garlic, and peppercorns over the cheeses. Add enough additional olive oil to completely cover. Marinate, covered, in a cool place for several hours or refrigerate for several days. *Serves 4 as an appetizer.*

CAPRINI PICCANTI
goat cheese marinated in oil and red pepper flakes

If Italian goat cheese, caprini, is available try it instead of the more readily available French or California goat cheeses. The Italian cheese is drier, less creamy, and slightly more acidic than the French or Californian, and as such is delicious marinated. If you do not want to marinate the cheese overnight, serve the goat cheese in the Italian manner: Sprinkle it with red pepper flakes and pour a bit of olive oil over.

2 small goat cheeses, or 2 Italian caprini

2–3 teaspoons red pepper flakes
Fruity olive oil to cover

Unwrap the cheeses and place in a small glass jar or in a small soufflé dish. Sprinkle red pepper flakes over the cheese and pour olive oil over to cover. Cover the jar or dish and set in a cool place to marinate for at least 24 hours. Serve with crostini (see page 9) or crusty peasant bread. Accompany with black olives. *Serves 4 to 6.*

PROSCIUTTO, FIGS, AND RICOTTA SALATA

A beautiful first course. Serve with quality breadsticks, the long thin variety, or crusty bread. We love the strong flavors of the prosciutto and ricotta salata in contrast with the intensely sweet flesh of the figs. The mint is an edible garnish, cool and fresh tasting. Follow with Shrimp Marinated in Wild Fennel (see page 194) or Simple Boiled Lobster (see page 201) with lemon or lime wedges.

12 fresh ripe figs, cut in half lengthwise
1 pound ricotta salata or feta cheese (see note), cut into ¾-inch dice

12 slices prosciutto
Fresh mint sprigs
Pepper mill

Arrange the figs, ricotta salata, and prosciutto on a platter. Garnish with the mint sprigs. Pass a pepper mill. *Serves 4.*

NOTE:

Ricotta salata is a firm, salted cheese made from sheep's milk, similar in texture to feta. It's available in most Italian specialty food shops.

TORTAS

layered cheese appetizers

"Tortas" layered with pesto, gorgonzola, smoked salmon, and other fillings are imported from the renowned gastronomia Peck in Milan, Italy. Found in many gourmet specialty shops, the layered cheese appetizers are very expensive and often show wear from the long journey. Tortas are easy and much less expensive to make at home. A show-stopper hors d'oeuvre, they are a welcome break from the brie and crackers routine. Try serving a variety of tortas at the same time. Use your imagination for fillings. For example, try layering with any combination of fresh herbs, smoked salmon, or saga blue cheese.

The master recipe which follows serves 20 as an hors d'oeuvre. To serve fewer people, cut the amounts for the cheese mixture and fillings in half and mold in a small cylindrical container such as an empty plastic ricotta container. Line the mold with cheesecloth as described in the master recipe and proceed as directed. The tapered height of the small mold looks beautiful and makes it possible to create many layers.

TORTA MASTER RECIPE

1 pound unsalted butter,   *1 cup Torta Filling*
     softened
1 pound cream cheese,
     softened

Mix the butter and cream cheese in an electric mixer until well combined. Line a 9 × 5-inch loaf pan with two layers of dampened cheesecloth with enough overhanging to cover the top. Alternate layers of cheese mixture and filling in the pan, starting and finishing with a cheese layer. Fold edges of cheesecloth over top and refrigerate at least 2 hours or until firm. Unmold by turning the pan onto a plate and gently tapping until the torta releases. Remove the pan and the cheesecloth. The torta can be made several days in advance and refrigerated. The longer the torta sits, the more the color and flavor of the filling will permeate the white cheese. *Serves 20 as an hors d'oeuvre.*

PESTO FILLING FOR TORTA

The amounts given in this pesto recipe are intended to produce a mixture much thicker than that usually used for dressing pasta.

*2½ cups fresh basil leaves,
    tightly packed*
⅓ cup olive oil
1 cup grated Parmesan cheese

½ cup pine nuts
*Coarse salt and freshly ground
    pepper to taste*
Fresh basil leaves for garnish

Process the basil in a food processor until finely chopped. With the machine running, add the olive oil, Parmesan, ¼ cup of the pine nuts, and salt and pepper. When layering the torta, sprinkle each layer of pesto with some of the remaining pine nuts. Decorate the unmolded torta with basil leaves and pine nuts.

NOTE:
Winter Pesto Two (see page 275) can also be used as the filling. CONTINUED

PESTO DI OLIVE FILLING
FOR TORTA

½ cup coarsely chopped
    walnuts
1 cup Pesto di Olive (see page 276)

Oil-cured black olives and
    lightly toasted whole
    walnuts for garnish

Lightly toast the walnuts in a skillet on top of the stove or in a preheated 350° oven for 5 to 7 minutes. The walnuts should be golden, not dark brown. When layering the torta, sprinkle each layer of Pesto di Olive with chopped walnuts. Decorate the unmolded torta with olives and whole walnuts.

HARD-COOKED EGGS AND WHOLE BASIL LEAVES

Nothing could be more simple to prepare than this fresh-looking, really exquisite dish. The eggs are circled with basil leaves to form flowers and served with coarse salt and fresh pepper. When preparing a dish of such simplicity, great care must be taken. The eggs must be meltingly tender, the basil leaves beautiful, large, and unblemished, the salt must be pure and taste of salt, and the pepper must be fresh and aromatic. Each ingredient is of equal importance.

6 hard-cooked eggs
12 perfect fresh basil leaves

Coarse salt
A pepper mill

Peel the eggs and cut in half crosswise. Trim a little of the egg white off each end so that the egg halves do not tip over when placed on end. Arrange the eggs on end on a platter, with basil leaves radiating out from each egg like petals. Crush the salt lightly with a pestle or the back of a spoon. Put in a small dish and place on the table along with the pepper mill. *Serves 6.*

MINT-STUFFED EGGS WITH LEMON MAYONNAISE

This makes an exuberant, pretty presentation with the colorful flecks of giardiniera set against the pale yellow mayonnaise. The rich flavors of hard-cooked egg and mayonnaise are offset by the tart, vinegary flavors of the giardiniera and capers.

6 hard-cooked eggs
1 teaspoon red wine vinegar
2 tablespoons olive oil
1 tablespoon finely chopped fresh mint leaves
1 small garlic clove, peeled and minced

Coarse salt and freshly ground pepper to taste
½ cup Lemon Mayonnaise (see page 265)
Capers
Giardiniera, mild
Fresh mint sprigs

Peel the eggs and halve lengthwise. Carefully remove the yolks. Reserve the egg whites. Combine the yolks with the vinegar, olive oil, mint and garlic in a small bowl and mix until well blended. Season with the salt and pepper. Mound the mixture neatly into the hollows in the reserved egg whites. Lightly cover the eggs with the Lemon Mayonnaise. Garnish each egg with capers and small pieces of giardiniera. Garnish the platter with mint sprigs. *Serves 6.*

FRITTATA WITH FOUR FLAVORS

A light dish with the sweet presence of herbs.

6–8 eggs
¼ cup grated Parmesan
    cheese
Coarse salt and freshly ground
    pepper to taste
2 teaspoons chopped fresh
    tarragon leaves, or ½
    teaspoon dried tarragon
    leaves, crumbled

1 tablespoon each chopped
    fresh mint leaves, fresh
    flat-leaf parsley, and fresh
    marjoram leaves, or 1
    teaspoon each dried mint
    leaves, basil leaves, and
    marjoram leaves,
    crumbled
2 tablespoons olive oil

Lightly beat the eggs in a bowl with the Parmesan, salt and pepper, and herbs. Heat the olive oil in a small, nonstick, ovenproof skillet. Swirl the oil in the pan to coat all sides. Add the egg mixture. Lower the heat.

TO COOK ALL FRITTATAS:

Cook slowly, stirring frequently, until the eggs have formed small curds and the frittata is firm except for the top. To cook the top, place the pan under a hot broiler or into a preheated 400° oven until the frittata browns lightly. Remove the pan from the broiler or oven. Let cool in the pan 1 or 2 minutes. Place a plate over the top of pan and invert the frittata onto it. Serve the frittata at room temperature, cut into wedges. *Serves 4.*

RICOTTA FRITTATA

Lightly beating the ricotta into the egg mixture helps the frittata puff and stay puffed. The cheese will form lovely white streaks throughout the eggs.

6–8 eggs
½ cup ricotta
¼ cup grated Parmesan
    cheese
2 tablespoons finely chopped
    fresh parsley

2 teaspoons chopped fresh
    thyme leaves, or ¾
    teaspoon dried whole
    thyme leaves, crumbled
Coarse salt and freshly ground
    pepper to taste
2 tablespoons olive oil

Lightly beat the eggs in a bowl with the ricotta, Parmesan, parsley, thyme, salt, and pepper. Heat the oil in a small, nonstick, ovenproof skillet. Swirl the oil in the pan to coat all sides. Add the egg mixture. Lower the heat. Cook and unmold according to the general frittata recipe (see page 104). Serve at room temperature, cut into wedges. *Serves 4.*

ZUCCHINI AND BASIL FRITTATA

The basil adds a light, sweet taste to this frittata. Shredding, salting, and squeezing the zucchini dry allows a very brief cooking time, thus reducing the amount of oil the zucchini absorbs.

1 pound small, firm zucchini
Coarse salt
4 tablespoons olive oil
3 garlic cloves, peeled and
    minced
6–8 eggs
¼ cup grated Parmesan
    cheese

¼ cup coarsely chopped fresh
    basil leaves, or 2
    teaspoons dried basil
    leaves, crumbled
Freshly ground pepper to taste

Trim the ends off the zucchini. Grate on the largest hole of 4-sided grater. Salt the zucchini, place in a colander, and let drain for 30 minutes. Press out the liquid. Heat 2 tablespoons of the olive oil in a small nonstick skillet. Sauté the garlic briefly. Add the zucchini and sauté 5 or 6 minutes over high heat until the excess moisture evaporates and the zucchini turns bright green. Let cool. Lightly beat the eggs in a bowl. Add the Parmesan, basil, cooked zucchini, salt, and pepper. Stir to combine. In a small, nonstick, ovenproof skillet, heat the remaining 2 tablespoons olive oil. Swirl the oil in the skillet to coat all sides. Add the egg-zucchini mixture. Lower the heat. Cook and unmold according to the general frittata recipe (see page 104). Serve at room temperature, cut into wedges. *Serves 4.*

ORANGE FRITTATA

The combination of orange and tomato flavors makes this frittata particularly unusual. Its fresh flavor is especially suited for brunches.

6 eggs

1 tablespoon dry sherry

3 tablespoons tomato sauce, or
    tomato purée

Coarse salt to taste

Pinch of cayenne pepper

2 tablespoons olive oil

2 oranges, preferably navel

Lightly beat the eggs, sherry, tomato sauce, salt, and cayenne pepper together in a bowl. Heat the oil in a small, nonstick, ovenproof skillet. Swirl the oil to coat all sides. Add the egg mixture to the skillet. Lower the heat. Cook and unmold according to the general frittata recipe (see page 104). Squeeze the juice of 1 orange over it. Cool to room temperature. Meanwhile, peel the second orange and remove as much of the white pith as is possible. Slip a sharp paring knife between the white membrane to release the individual orange segments. Garnish the cooled frittata by arranging the segments around the edge. *Serves 4.*

PASTA FRITTATA

This is the perfect way to use up leftover pasta of any shape that has been served with a tomato sauce. We never have any left after a meal and must make fresh. Whichever way you begin, the result is a hearty and satisfying meal. The color of the tomatoes seeps into the eggs, creating a beautiful red-orange color. It's fun to cut into the frittata and see the different patterns that different shapes of pasta create.

6–8 eggs
½ cup grated Parmesan cheese
Coarse salt and freshly ground
     pepper to taste
2 tablespoons olive oil

1 garlic clove, peeled and
     finely chopped
2 cups cooked pasta with
     marinara or other red
     sauce

Lightly beat the eggs with the Parmesan, salt, and pepper in a bowl. Heat the oil in a small, nonstick, ovenproof skillet. Sauté the garlic briefly. Add the pasta and heat through. It is all the better if some of the noodles get crispy; it improves the texture. Beat the eggs briefly again and pour over the pasta in the skillet. Lower the heat. Cook and unmold according to the general frittata recipe (see page 104). Serve at room temperature, cut into wedges. *Serves 4.*

PARSLEY FRITTATA WITH BREAD CRUMBS

The flavor of parsley works well with that of eggs, and the bread crumbs give this frittata a dense, firm texture. Parsley frittata is a favorite food of Federico Fellini.

6–8 eggs
1 cup loosely packed fresh
     parsley leaves, finely
     minced
2 garlic cloves, peeled and
     minced
¼ cup grated Parmesan cheese

3 tablespoons homemade
     bread crumbs
Coarse salt and freshly ground
     pepper to taste
2 tablespoons olive oil

Lightly beat the eggs in a bowl. Add the parsley, garlic, Parmesan, bread crumbs, salt, and pepper. Stir to combine. Heat the oil in a small, nonstick, ovenproof skillet. Swirl the oil in the skillet to coat all sides. Add the egg-parsley mixture. Lower the heat. Cook and unmold according to the general frittata recipe (see page 104). Serve at room temperature, cut into wedges. *Serves 4.*

S M O K E D   S A L M O N   F R I T T A T A   W I T H   C A V I A R

This is a beautiful, elegant frittata which can be served not only for a brunch or late supper, but also as an appetizer, cut into thin slices. The smoky flavor of the fish permeates the eggs, making the dish especially rich and savory.

6–8 eggs
Coarse salt and freshly ground
   pepper to taste
2 tablespoons minced fresh chives
⅛ pound smoked salmon (lox),
   cut into slivers

2 tablespoons olive oil
4 ounces sour cream
4–6 ounces salmon eggs, or
   golden caviar (whitefish
   roe)

Lightly beat the eggs in a bowl with salt and pepper. Add the chives and smoked salmon. Stir to combine. In a small, nonstick, ovenproof skillet, heat the olive oil. Swirl the oil in the skillet to coat all sides. Add the egg-salmon mixture. Lower the heat. Cook and unmold according to the general frittata recipe (see page 104). Serve at room temperature, cut into wedges. Garnish each serving with a dollop of sour cream and a spoonful of caviar. *Serves 4.*

WILD MUSHROOM AND PROSCIUTTO FRITTATA

A frittata with the deep, rich, woodsy taste of shiitake mushrooms.

¼ pound wild mushrooms, such as shiitake mushrooms

5 tablespoons olive oil

1 garlic clove, peeled and minced

Coarse salt and freshly ground pepper to taste

6–8 eggs

¼ cup grated Parmesan cheese

1 tablespoon coarsely chopped fresh parsley

4 thin slices prosciutto, chopped

Slice the mushrooms into thin strips. Gently heat 3 tablespoons of the olive oil in a medium saucepan. Sauté the garlic briefly. Add the mushrooms and sauté for 2 minutes, tossing the mushrooms in the oil. Add the salt and pepper. Set aside to cool. Lightly beat the eggs in a bowl. Add the Parmesan, parsley, prosciutto, and cooled mushrooms. Stir to combine. Season with salt and pepper, remembering that the prosciutto and Parmesan are salty. Heat the remaining 2 tablespoons olive oil in a small, nonstick, ovenproof skillet. Swirl the oil in the skillet to coat all sides. Add egg mixture. Lower the heat. Cook and unmold according to the general frittata recipe (see page 104). Serve at room temperature, cut into wedges. *Serves 4.*

FRITTATA SPAGNOLA

spanish frittata

The amounts in this recipe can be used as a guide to increase any other frittata recipe found in the chapter. This frittata is hearty and satisfying breakfast or luncheon food for a large group.

20 eggs
Coarse salt and freshly ground
pepper to taste
½ cup olive oil combined with
½ cup vegetable oil

8 large all-purpose potatoes,
peeled and sliced
2 large onions, peeled and
sliced

Lightly beat the eggs in a large bowl and season with salt and pepper. Heat half the oil mixture in a medium nonstick skillet. When the oil is hot, add the potatoes and onions and sauté gently, stirring frequently, until the potatoes are tender but firm. Remove from the heat and add the potato mixture to the eggs. Mix thoroughly. Heat the remaining oil in a large, nonstick, ovenproof skillet. Pour the potato-egg mixture into the skillet. Lower the heat, cover the skillet, and cook gently until the mixture is firm. Use the cover of the skillet or a plate to turn the frittata over. Slip it back into the pan and brown the other side. Alternatively, if the skillet is ovenproof, leave the frittata in the skillet and brown the top under the broiler. Let the frittata cool in the pan 1 or 2 minutes. Slide from the skillet onto a platter. Serve at room temperature, sliced like pie. *Serves 15.*

savory tarts

PASTA FROLLA
flaky pastry dough

Pasta Frolla is a versatile, fairly simple tart crust well suited to the moist nature of savory fillings. The dough stores well in the refrigerator up to one week, and uncooked prepared tart shells freeze beautifully up to one month.

When making a tart shell, it is important to remember that the character of the crust will be determined by the balance of the ingredients. Too much flour toughens the dough; too much water makes an unappealingly soggy crust; and too much butter or vegetable shortening will cause the crust to crumble. Handle the dough as little as possible. If the ingredients are well chilled and the dough is worked lightly, it may not be necessary to refrigerate the dough to allow it to rest. If the dough appears elastic, it is necessary to wrap it in plastic wrap and refrigerate for one hour in order to tenderize the dough. To facilitate the rolling of chilled dough, remove it from the refrigerator fifteen minutes or so before preparing the tart shell.

Using all butter lends a fine, buttery taste to the crust. Many people, however, feel that substituting a small amount of vegetable shortening for the butter makes a flakier crust. Given the highly flavored nature of most savory tart fillings, it is almost impossible to taste the difference in a crust which includes vegetable shortening. In the following recipe, we advocate using all butter; but if you wish, you may substitute up to 4 tablespoons of vegetable shortening for an equal amount of butter.

2½ cups all-purpose flour
¼ teaspoon salt

2 sticks (8 ounces) cold unsalted butter, cut into pieces
6 tablespoons ice water

Combine the flour and salt in a bowl. Stir to mix. Add the butter pieces. Rapidly cut the butter into flour with your fingertips or two knives, until the mixture resembles coarse meal. Gradually add the water and mix the dough with a fork until it gathers together. Gather the dough together into a ball, wrap in plastic wrap, and refrigerate at least 1 hour. When ready to make a tart, remove the dough from the refrigerator, unwrap it, and place on a lightly floured board. Hit the dough a few times with a rolling pin to soften it. Roll out in a circular shape to a thickness of between ⅛ and ¼ inch. Gently lift the dough up on the rolling pin and ease into the tart pan. Firmly press the dough into the pan without stretching. Trim the top by rolling over it with the rolling pin. Refrigerate at least 30 minutes or until ready to use. To partially prebake the shell, line the crust with aluminum foil. Fill with pie weights, rice, or dried beans. Bake in a preheated 400° oven for 15 minutes. Remove from the oven and lift out the aluminum foil and weights. Prick the bottom with a fork. Bake another 3 to 5 minutes to dry the pastry. Let cool. *Makes enough for a 10-inch tart.*

SOFT TART DOUGH

This rich egg dough is easy to work with as it patches easily. Its very rustic, country simplicity complements highly flavored fillings such as in the Torta Rustica (see page 120) and the Tortellini Tart (see page 117). A beautiful feature of the dough is its smooth, matte finish when baked without an egg wash.

4 cups all-purpose flour
1 teaspoon salt
2 sticks (8 ounces) cold unsalted butter, cut into pieces

2 eggs
2 egg yolks
⅓ cup milk, approximately

BY HAND:
Combine the flour and salt in a large bowl. Make a well in the center and add the butter, eggs, and yolks. Lightly blend the butter mixture with fingertips. With a knife or pastry blender, cut the dry ingredients into the wet ingredients until the dough is crumbly. Gradually add

the milk, tossing with a fork, until the dough comes together. The dough will be soft. Gather into a ball. Wrap the dough in plastic wrap and refrigerate at least 1 hour or up to 2 or 3 days. When ready to roll the dough, place it on parchment, wax paper, aluminum foil, or plastic wrap to facilitate handling.

FOOD PROCESSOR:
Combine the flour, salt, and butter in a food processor fitted with a metal blade. Process with short pulses until the mixture is crumbly. Add the eggs and yolks with short pulses; do not overmix. Add milk gradually with short pulses until dough begins to clump. Remove the dough and proceed as above. *Makes enough for a 14-inch tart.*

PIZZA DOUGH

Pizza dough has a wonderful rough quality which when used with certain simple, highly flavored fillings creates a homey, rustic treat that is beautifully simple in appearance and satisfying to eat.

1 package active dry yeast
2¼ cups warm water
4½ cups all-purpose flour,
  and more as needed

2 teaspoons salt
2 tablespoons olive oil

Add the yeast to the warm water in a small bowl. Let dissolve. Combine the flour and salt in another bowl. Stir to mix. Make a well in the center of the flour. Pour in the dissolved yeast and oil. Stir with a wooden spoon or fingers until the dough forms. Turn the dough out onto a floured board and knead 10 to 15 minutes, adding flour as needed to prevent sticking, until the dough is smooth and elastic. Place the dough in a lightly oiled bowl, turn to coat, and cover with a damp cloth. Place the bowl in a warm, draft-free spot for 2 hours or until the dough doubles in bulk. Punch down the dough, and turn out onto a floured board. Knead lightly. Reserve one-third of the dough for the top crust. Roll the dough with a rolling pin into a large circle and place into a 10-inch springform pan letting the edges overhang by one inch. Place the filling into the dough-lined pan. Roll the remaining dough into a circle the size of the form. It should be approximately ¼ inch thick. Place the circle on top of the filling and bring the 1-inch overhang over the edges of the circle, pinching together. The tart is now ready to be baked.

TORTELLINI TART

Made over one or two days, the final assembly of this tart is fast and simple. The result is an impressive meal that is simple and satisfying. Keep accompaniments light and serve with a good red wine. If possible, use fresh tortellini; frozen tortellini are a good substitute. Avoid the dried variety.

TORTELLINI:

1½ pounds meat-stuffed tortellini

1–2 tablespoons olive oil

Boil tortellini in an abundant amount of salted water in a large pot for 12 minutes or until tender yet still firm to the bite. Drain the tortellini in a colander and gently rinse under cold running water until they feel cool to the touch. Drain and place in a bowl. Toss 1 or 2 tablespoons of olive oil with the tortellini to keep them from sticking together. Set the tortellini aside.

SAUCE:

1 ounce dried porcini mushrooms

2 celery stalks, peeled and minced

2 carrots, peeled, trimmed, and minced

1 onion, peeled and minced

1 garlic clove, peeled and minced

3 tablespoons olive oil

2 pounds ground chuck

½ pound sweet Italian sausage

1 cup red wine

2 tablespoons minced fresh parsley leaves

2–3 fresh sage leaves, or ½ teaspoon dried sage leaves, crumbled

1 can (14 ounces) tomato sauce

2 cups broth or water

Cover the porcini mushrooms with warm water in a small bowl. Let soak 30 minutes or until soft. Meanwhile, sauté the celery, carrots, onion, and garlic in the olive oil in a skillet over low heat until soft. Add the ground meat and sausage and let brown. Add the wine and let cook over high heat until it evaporates. Add the parsley, sage, tomato sauce, and broth. Stir to mix. Drain the porcini mushrooms, checking to be sure they are free of dirt. Add to the sauce. Simmer the sauce over low heat until it reduces and is thick enough to grab the spoon. Set the sauce aside to cool.

BÉCHAMEL:

½ stick (2 ounces) unsalted butter

3 tablespoons all-purpose flour

2 cups hot milk

Coarse salt and freshly ground pepper to taste

Melt the butter in a small saucepan over low heat. Add the flour and stir to form a smooth paste. Heat the milk in a separate saucepan. When it is hot but not boiling, pour it into the roux (butter-flour mixture), stirring constantly with a whisk or wooden spoon. Cook over low heat until the sauce thickens and the flour taste is gone. Add salt and pepper. Set aside.

CRUST:

1 recipe Soft Tart Dough (see
    page 115)

1 egg beaten with 2
    tablespoons milk

To assemble the tart, first mix the tortellini and sauce together in a bowl. Roll out two-thirds of the Soft Tart Dough on parchment, wax paper, aluminum foil, or plastic wrap in a circle about 14 inches in diameter. Line a medium mixing bowl with plastic wrap. Invert the 14-inch circle of dough into the bowl. Peel off the paper or plastic wrap and pat the dough against the sides of the bowl.

Place half the sauced tortellini into the dough-lined bowl, being careful to extend the layer to the edge of the dough. Using a rubber spatula, cover the tortellini with the cooled béchamel. Top the béchamel with the remaining tortellini, again being careful to extend the layer to the edge of the dough. Roll out the remaining dough on parchment, wax paper, aluminum foil, or plastic wrap into a circle large enough to cover the filling. Invert the dough onto the tart filling. Peel off the paper or plastic wrap and trim the edges of the circle (which will become the bottom crust). Brush the edge of the circle with the egg wash and fold over the extra dough from the larger circle (which will be the top of the tart). Make sure the edges are well sealed. Carefully invert the tart onto a baking sheet and remove the bowl. Peel off the plastic wrap that lined the bowl.

CONTINUED

Bake the tart in a preheated 375° oven for about 40 minutes or until the crust is a deep golden brown. If you desire a sheen to the crust, brush it with the egg wash before placing it in the oven and once or twice during baking. Serve the tart at room temperature. Cut into pie-shaped wedges to serve. *Serves 10 to 12.*

TORTA RUSTICA
rustic country tart

Country cooking that pleases the most sophisticated palate. Cutting into the tart reveals a brilliant mosaic of colors. To make even more substantial, add cubes of Arista (see page 220). Or, if Black Forest ham proves difficult to find, substitute any high-quality smoked meat.

6 packages (10 ounces each) frozen chopped spinach
1 tablespoon butter
1 tablespoon olive oil
1 small onion, peeled and minced
4 eggs
1 cup grated Parmesan cheese
½ cup bread crumbs
Coarse salt and freshly ground pepper to taste

4 large red bell peppers, or a 1-pound can good quality peeled red peppers
1 recipe Soft Tart Dough (see page 115)
½ pound Italian fontina, rind removed, sliced
½ pound Black Forest ham, sliced ⅛ inch thick
1 egg beaten with 2 tablespoons milk

Cook the spinach according to the package directions. Drain in a colander and rinse under cold water to cool. Drain the spinach and with your hands squeeze out the excess moisture. The spinach should be almost completely dry. Set aside. Heat the butter and oil together in a small skillet. Sauté the minced onion until it becomes translucent and begins to color. Mix together the spinach, sautéed onion, eggs, Parmesan, bread crumbs, salt, and pepper in a bowl. Set aside.

To peel the peppers, place them over a gas burner or under a broiler and turn with tongs until they are blackened all over. Place them in plastic bags, close the top, and let them sweat for 10 minutes. Remove the peppers from the plastic bag and rinse the skins off under cold running water. Lay on paper towels to dry. Carefully remove the stems, open the peppers, and discard the seeds and white ribs. Cut the peppers to lie flat in one piece. Set aside.

To assemble the tart, roll out two-thirds of the Soft Tart Dough on parchment, wax paper, aluminum foil, or plastic wrap into a circle approximately 14 inches in diameter. Line a medium mixing bowl with plastic wrap. Invert the 14-inch circle of dough into the bowl. Peel off the paper or plastic wrap and pat the dough against the sides of the bowl. Now begin to layer the ingredients. First, place a thin layer of spinach mixture, then a layer of red pepper, fontina, and ham. Continue layering in a pattern you like, but finish with a layer of spinach at least ½ inch thick.

Roll out the remaining dough on parchment, wax paper, aluminum foil, or plastic wrap into a circle large enough to cover the filling. Invert the dough onto the tart filling and peel off the paper or plastic wrap. Trim the edges of the circle (which will become the bottom crust). Brush the edge of the circle with the egg wash and fold over the extra dough from the larger circle (which will be the top of the tart). Make sure the edges are well sealed. Carefully invert the tart onto a baking sheet and remove the bowl. Peel off the plastic wrap that lined the bowl.

CONTINUED

Bake the tart in a preheated 375° oven for approximately 40 minutes or until the crust is a deep golden brown. If you desire a sheen to the crust, brush it with the egg wash before placing it in the oven and once or twice during baking. Serve the tart at room temperature, cut into pie-shaped wedges. *Serves 10 to 12.*

MUSHROOM TART

If wild, fresh, deep-flavored mushrooms like porcini or shiitake are available, by all means substitute up to half a pound for the ounce of dried. Adding a bit of fresh or dried thyme to the dough intensifies the woodsy flavor of the tart.

1 ounce dried porcini or shiitake mushrooms
1½ pounds fresh white or brown mushrooms
4 tablespoons butter
4 tablespoons olive oil
Coarse salt and freshly ground pepper to taste
½ pound dandelion greens
1 garlic clove, peeled and minced
3 sprigs fresh thyme, or ½ teaspoon dried thyme leaves, crumbled

¼ cup Madeira or port
2 tablespoons bread crumbs
1 unbaked 10-inch Pasta Frolla tart shell (see page 113)
2 ounces prosciutto, cut a little thick
1 ounce Gruyère cheese, grated
6 eggs
2 cups half and half

Place the dried mushrooms in a bowl and cover with very warm water. Set aside for at least 30 minutes or until the mushrooms soften. Clean the fresh mushrooms by wiping with a damp cloth. Trim off the woody stems and slice the mushrooms. Heat 2 tablespoons of the butter and 2 tablespoons of the oil together in a medium skillet. Add the sliced fresh mushrooms, salt, and pepper. Sauté over moderate heat just until the mushrooms begin to wilt; do not overcook. Remove from the heat and turn into a strainer to drain.

Wash the dandelion greens well. Dry and coarsely chop. Heat 1 tablespoon each of the butter and olive oil in a small skillet. Add the minced garlic and thyme. Stir over low heat until you smell the herb. Add the dandelion greens. Sauté over moderate heat just until the greens wilt. Turn into a clean strainer to drain.

Drain the dried mushrooms, reserving 2 tablespoons of the soaking liquid. Check the mushrooms to be sure they are free from sand. Dry them. Heat 1 tablespoon each of the butter and oil in a small skillet. Add the dried mushrooms and sauté gently. Add the Madeira or port and cook until the wine evaporates.

Line a 10 by 2-inch removable-bottom round tart pan with the pastry. To assemble the tart, scatter the bread crumbs over the bottom of the pastry shell. Add the greens, both types of mushrooms, the prosciutto, and grated Gruyère. Lightly beat together the eggs with half and half in a bowl. Pour over the other ingredients in the shell. Bake the tart in the middle of a preheated 375° oven for about 40 minutes. The tart will puff slightly. It is done when a knife inserted comes out clean. Cool at least 10 minutes before removing from tart pan. Serve at room temperature, cut into pie-shaped wedges. *Serves 10 to 12.*

RICOTTA AND BASIL TART

The classic combination of flavors in this lovely pale green tart makes it light and flavorful.

2 cups fresh basil leaves,
    tightly packed
2 tablespoons minced fresh
    flat-leaf parsley
2 tablespoons fruity olive oil
2 containers (15 ounces each)
    ricotta
¼ cup grated Parmesan
    cheese, or mixed grated
    Romano and grated
    Parmesan cheeses

2 eggs
⅛ cup oil-cured black olives,
    pitted
Coarse salt to taste
1 partially baked 10-inch
    Pasta Frolla tart shell (see
    page 113)

Combine the basil and parsley in a food processor. Process until coarsely chopped. Add the oil, ricotta, and grated cheese to the work bowl. Process just until mixed. Beat in the eggs. Stir in the olives. Line a 10 by ¾-inch pie plate or removable-bottom round tart pan with pastry and partially bake the shell according to the directions on page 115. To assemble the tart, pour the ricotta mixture into the shell. Evenly distribute it around the shell with a spatula. Bake the tart in a preheated 375° oven for about 35 minutes or until the tart puffs slightly and a knife inserted comes out clean. Serve at room temperature. *Serves 6 to 8.*

TORTA NIZZA

This country tart is perfect picnic fare. Serve as a first course to Rosemary Chicken (see page 225).

6 large, firm Bermuda onions, peeled

3 tablespoons olive oil

2 teaspoons dried oregano leaves, crumbled

Coarse salt and freshly ground pepper to taste

2 firm, ripe tomatoes

1 recipe Pizza Dough (see page 116)

2 tablespoons bread crumbs

¼ cup Niçoise olives, pitted

Slice 4 of the onions crosswise into thin slices. Gently sauté the onion in the olive oil in a large skillet with the oregano, salt, and pepper until the onion becomes translucent and begins to color, about 10 to 15 minutes. Turn into a strainer to drain. Wash and stem the tomatoes. Cut into ½-inch slices and set on paper towels to drain. Meanwhile, cut the remaining 2 onions crosswise into ½-inch-thick slices. Line a 10-inch springform pan with three-quarters of the pizza dough. Roll out remaining dough into an 11-inch circle for top crust.

To assemble the tart, sprinkle the bread crumbs over the bottom of the tart shell. Place enough raw slices of onion over the crumbs to cover the bottom without overlapping. Cover the onion with some of the drained sautéed onions. Place a layer of tomato slices over the cooked onion and sprinkle with some of the olives. Continue layering with uncooked onion slices, sautéed onion, tomato, and olives until all the ingredients are used. Place the pizza dough circle over the filling and bring the overhang from the dough in the pan over the edges of the circle, pinching together. Bake the tart in a preheated 375° oven for approximately 45 minutes or until the tart is puffed and deep golden brown. Let cool for 10 minutes. Remove the springform pan. Place on a wire rack to cool. Serve at room temperature, cut into pie-shaped wedges. *Serves 8 to 10.*

C H E E S E   T A R T

This easy to make savory tart is a good complement to cocktails. Most quality French bakeries sell fresh puff pastry dough by the pound. Always keep a supply on hand in your freezer to make a quality tart in little time.

1½ pounds puff pastry dough
½ pound sweet gorgonzola
    cheese, trimmed of rind
5 ounces goat cheese

1 egg yolk
Freshly ground pepper to taste
1 egg beaten with 1 tablespoon
    milk

Divide the puff pastry in half. Roll out each piece on a lightly floured board into about a 10-inch square. Refrigerate until ready to use. Mix together the gorgonzola, goat cheese, and egg yolk with a fork in a small bowl. Add the pepper. Remove the dough from the refrigerator. Leaving an inch border on all sides, spread the cheese mixture evenly with a rubber spatula over one square of dough. Brush the border with the egg wash. Place the second puff paste square over the first. Crimp the edges of the tart together with a fork. Brush the tart with the egg wash. Bake on a baking sheet in a preheated 425° oven for about 15 minutes or until the tart is puffed and golden brown. Serve at room temperature. *Serves 6 as a light entrée, or 10 as an appetizer.*

VEAL-STUFFED QUAIL TART

2–3 tart apples, such as
   Granny Smith, cored and
   cut into ¼-inch-thick
   slices
4 tablespoons unsalted butter
1 tablespoon oil
2 pounds ground veal
1 teaspoon dried thyme leaves,
   crumbled
1 shallot, peeled and coarsely
   chopped

1–2 tablespoons Cognac
1 egg
Coarse salt and freshly ground
   pepper to taste
¼–½ cup heavy cream
6 quail, boned
3 pounds puff pastry dough
1 egg beaten with 2
   tablespoons milk

Sauté the apple slices in the butter and oil in a skillet over medium heat until nearly soft, about 15 minutes. They will cook further in the tart. Set aside. To make the stuffing for quail, combine the veal, thyme, shallot, Cognac, egg, salt, and pepper in a food processor. Process to blend. With the machine running, add just enough cream to lighten the mixture. Loosely stuff the quail with the veal mixture, using large toothpicks to secure the stuffing. Bake the quail on a baking sheet in a preheated 375° oven for 10 minutes. Let cool to room temperature.

To assemble the tart, roll out 2 circles of puff pastry dough, one 12 inches in diameter, one 16 inches. Place the 12-inch circle on a baking sheet. Arrange the apple slices on the 12-inch circle, leaving a ½-inch border. Arrange the cooled, stuffed quail on the apples. Cut a vent in the center of the 16-inch circle of pastry with the tip of a pastry tube. Brush the edge of the 16-inch pastry circle with the egg wash. Drape the circle, glazed side down, over the quail. Seal the edges of the tart with the tines of a fork and brush the entire pastry with the egg wash. Bake in a preheated 425° oven for 10 minutes. Then lower the heat to 375°. Bake for an additional 10 to 15 minutes or until the dough is puffed and golden brown and the filling is bubbling. Serve at room temperature. *Serves 6.*

TIMBALLO DI MELANZANE
eggplant timbale

Slices of fried eggplant line the bottom and sides of this tart. The eggs give a firm, cake-like texture which makes serving easier. The rich creaminess of the eggplant makes this dish satisfying as a main course. Do not substitute other oils for the olive oil as its flavor is an important aspect of the timbale.

2½–3 eggplants, stem end trimmed and cut lengthwise into ⅓-inch-thick slices
Coarse salt
1 recipe Tomato-Basil Sauce (see page 271)

1 cup all-purpose flour
Olive oil for frying
1 cup grated Parmesan cheese
½ pound mozzarella, shredded
3 large eggs, lightly beaten

Lay the eggplant slices out on paper towels and salt them generously. Let sit for at least 15 minutes or until beads of water gather on top of the slices. Meanwhile, make the Tomato-Basil Sauce according to the directions on page 271. Cook the sauce longer than directed, until it is a very thick purée. Set aside to cool. Dry the eggplant slices with paper towels. Lightly dredge the slices in flour, shaking off the excess. Pour the olive oil to a depth of ¼ inch in a heavy skillet with high sides. Heat until the oil is hot but not smoking. Fry the eggplant slices in 1 layer, turning once as they brown and adding more oil as necessary. As the slices brown, remove with tongs to paper towels to drain.

To assemble the timbale, arrange just enough eggplant slices in an overlapping radial pattern to cover the bottom of a 2-quart soufflé dish; the eggplant will come partially up the sides. Place more eggplant slices, vertically, in a slightly overlapping fashion, up and over the sides of the dish, and overhanging the edge. Cover the bottom layer of eggplant with 3 to 4 tablespoons of the sauce. Sprinkle with a few tablespoons of grated Parmesan and shredded mozzarella. Cover the sauce with a layer of eggplant, cutting the pieces to fit if necessary. Continue layering with sauce, Parmesan, mozzarella, and eggplant until all the eggplant slices are used. End with eggplant, sauce, and Parmesan, no mozzarella. Make incisions with a knife through the layers of eggplant. Pour the beaten eggs over the layered eggplant, making sure the eggs seep through and around the layers. To create the bottom layer, fold over the eggplant slices from the sides. Bake in a preheated 350° oven for 40 minutes or until the egg is set and the timbale is bubbling hot. Let cool at least 15 minutes before unmolding. Unmold timbale onto a serving plate and serve at room temperature. *Serves 8 to 10 as a vegetable, 6 to 8 as a main course.*

GRATTÓ DI PATATE

potato torta

The ultimate in rustic fare, this generous potato torta has a crisp, bread crumb coating with the strong flavors of cheese and salami as an accent to the mild and creamy potatoes. Thin bands of light tomato sauce create a pretty color contrast and add a touch of sweetness. The torta can be made several days ahead.

½ medium onion, finely chopped
6 tablespoons olive oil
2 cups canned Italian tomatoes with juice, tomatoes seeded and coarsely chopped
Coarse salt and freshly ground pepper to taste
8 large all-purpose potatoes, boiled and peeled

3 eggs, lightly beaten
1 cup coarsely chopped salami
1 cup diced mozzarella
¾ cup diced smoked provolone, or scamorza, skin removed
½ cup grated Parmesan cheese
½ cup chopped fresh parsley
2 tablespoons butter
1 cup bread crumbs

Sauté the onion in 3 tablespoons olive oil in a skillet over low heat until golden, about 3 to 4 minutes. Add the tomatoes, salt, and pepper. Cook over medium heat until the tomato sauce is thick and dry. Put potatoes through a ricer or mash in a bowl with a fork until smooth. Combine the potatoes with the eggs, salami, mozzarella, smoked provolone, Parmesan and parsley. Mix well.

Generously butter a 9 × 2½-inch springform pan. Coat heavily with bread crumbs, reserving some for the top. Spread one-third of the potato mixture evenly in the bottom of the pan. Spread half the tomato sauce over the potatoes. Spread another third of the potato mixture evenly over the tomato sauce. Repeat with the remaining tomato sauce and the potato mixture. Smooth the top. Sprinkle with the remaining bread crumbs. Drizzle with the remaining 3 tablespoons olive oil. Place on a baking sheet. Bake in a preheated 350° degree oven for 1 to 1¼ hours or until the top is crusty and brown. Let cool completely at room temperature. Refrigerate for several hours or overnight to make slicing easier. *Serves 8 very generously, or 12 as part of a buffet.*

S A R T Ù

r i c e   t i m b a l e   w i t h   v e a l   m e a t b a l l s

This savory, filling tart is a lovely centerpiece to a simple dinner, followed with a green leaf salad and fruit for dessert. A simple dish with many steps, its preparation is made easier over one or two days. Make the sauce as much as two days ahead, and the rice mixture and filling the day you plan to serve.

CONTINUED

TOMATO SAUCE:

1 garlic clove, peeled and
  minced

½ medium onion, peeled and
  minced

½ pound mushrooms, trimmed
  and sliced

2 zucchini, trimmed and cut
  into ¼-inch rounds

2 carrots, peeled, trimmed,
  and cut into ¼-inch
  rounds

3 tablespoons olive oil

1 can (28 ounces) Italian
  tomatoes

½ cup fresh parsley leaves

2–3 fresh basil leaves, minced,
  or 1 teaspoon dried basil
  leaves, crumbled

Sauté the garlic, onion, mushrooms, zucchini, and carrots in the oil in a large skillet until they just begin to color, about 4 to 5 minutes. Meanwhile, purée the tomatoes with their juice in a food processor or blender. Add the tomato purée to vegetables. Add the parsley and basil. Cook over moderately high heat for 5 minutes. Add the meatballs and chicken livers to the sauce. Continue cooking until the sauce thickens. Remove the meatballs and livers and set aside. The sauce should be very dense and not runny; cook longer if necessary. Reserve 1 cup of the Tomato Sauce for rice mixture.

CRUST:

3 cups long-grain white rice

4 tablespoons unsalted butter

⅔ cup grated Parmesan
  cheese

1 cup Tomato Sauce

2 eggs, lightly beaten

Cook the rice in an abundant amount of boiling salted water until tender, about 15 minutes. Drain thoroughly and place in bowl. Add the butter, Parmesan, thickened Tomato Sauce, and the eggs. Beat until thoroughly mixed. Set aside to cool.

FILLING:

3 slices (½ inch) French or
    Italian bread
½ cup milk
1 pound ground veal
Coarse salt and freshly ground
    pepper to taste

2 tablespoons olive oil
½ pound chicken livers,
    cleaned and cut in
    quarters

Soften the bread in the milk in a small bowl, 2 to 3 minutes. Squeeze dry. Mix the veal with the bread, salt, and pepper in a bowl. Pinch off the veal mixture into marble-size balls. Do not worry about making them perfectly round. Sauté the meatballs, working in batches if necessary, in the olive oil in a skillet until lightly browned. Lightly sauté the chicken liver in the oil just until firm, about 2 to 3 minutes.

TO ASSEMBLE TIMBALE:

Lightly butter an 8-inch springform pan. Lightly coat with the bread crumbs. Discard any excess. Press the Crust or rice mixture into bottom and sides of the springform pan as you would for a graham cracker crust. Do not build up the sides more than ½ inch. Reserve about 1½ cups of rice mixture for the top crust. Fill the rice crust with the mixture of meatballs, chicken livers, and tomato sauce. Cover the filling with the reserved rice mixture, making certain to bring the sides and top together. Place the timbale on a cookie sheet and bake in a preheated 375° oven for about 45 minutes to 1 hour or until the rice begins to color and is firm to the touch. Let cool at least 15 minutes in the springform pan before unmolding. Serve at room temperature. Cut into pie-shaped wedges to serve. *Serves 8.*

vegetables

SIMPLE ARTICHOKES

One of the great imponderables is who on earth was the first person to attempt to eat the artichoke? For we surely owe a debt to this brave soul who first approached the spring thistle. Here in America it seems that we are often intimidated by its fibrous nature, preferring to serve it cooked until the meaty heart has reached a spongy texture. We have often seen intrepid Europeans attack the vegetable in its natural raw state, slicing off bits from the tender base and stem to munch. Unfortunately, the beautifully small and tender European artichoke bears little resemblance to the sturdy varieties commercial growers in the United States seem to favor. There are differences, however, among our varieties to be aware of when selecting your artichokes. Look for those that are large for stuffing, small and tender for salads, and always, if you can find them, those with a purple blush at the tips with no hint of dryness. What follows is a simple, basic recipe that can be accompanied by an almost infinite variety of sauces, such as Basil Mayonnaise (see page 266) or Anchovy Dressing (see page 264).

6 artichokes　　　　　　　　　　*1 small bay leaf*
2 lemons, halved

Snap off the tough, outer leaves from the artichokes. As you finish trimming each artichoke, rub with a lemon half to prevent discoloration. Trim the stems if very long. Cut off the tapered tops by about 2 inches. With a scissors, cut off the sharp thistles from each artichoke leaf, if desired. Cut the artichokes in half lengthwise. Drop the artichokes into salted boiling water to cover in a saucepan. Squeeze the lemon juice into the water and add the lemon shells. Add the bay leaf. Turn the heat down so that the water is at an active simmer and cook the artichokes for about 20 to 30 minutes. They are cooked when a leaf can be easily pulled away or a sharp knife easily pierces the heart. Lift the artichokes out of the boiling water with a slotted spoon and plunge them immediately into a large bowl of ice water. Let the artichokes sit in the ice water until they are cool to the touch. Remove from the water and drain on paper towels. Using a spoon, carefully scrape away and discard the fuzzy choke from the artichoke heart. The artichokes are now ready to serve, garnished with the sauce of your choice. *Serves 6.*

BREAD-STUFFED ARTICHOKES

The garlicky piquant bread stuffing turns the artichoke into a light but filling meal. To serve as a first course we recommend cutting the stuffed artichoke in half. This is an unusual dish in that the stuffing, a mixture akin to a bread salad, is added after the artichoke is cooked.

6 artichokes
1 loaf of day-old, good-quality
*   Italian or French bread*
2 tomatoes, peeled, seeded,
*   and diced*
1 garlic clove, peeled and
*   minced*

2–3 tablespoons olive oil
2–3 tablespoons red wine
*   vinegar*
Coarse salt and freshly ground
*   pepper to taste*

Prepare artichokes as directed in Simple Artichokes (see opposite), leaving them whole. Remove the fuzzy chokes after cooking. If the crust of the bread is very thick, cut it off. Soak bread in about 1 cup of water. Squeeze it dry. Chop the bread coarsely and place in a large bowl. Add tomatoes, garlic, olive oil, vinegar, salt, and pepper to taste. Stir to combine. Carefully spread the artichoke leaves apart to make room for the stuffing. Using your fingers, place 3 tablespoons bread mixture loosely in the center cavity of each artichoke. Stuff the remaining bread mixture between the leaves of the artichokes. *Serves 6.*

ARTICHOKES ROMAN-STYLE

People always rave about these rich-tasting and meaty artichokes flavored with mint and garlic. Look for heavy artichokes with stems. Cleaned according to the directions, the whole artichoke is completely edible including the stem. Provide bread to soak up the savory juices. When served whole, this dish is good as a first course. To present the artichoke in a buffet style, however, prepare them as indicated, but first quarter the vegetable, remove the choke, and then braise with the herbs.

1 lemon, halved
4 large artichokes with stems
Coarse salt to taste
¼ cup fresh mint leaves,
*   chopped, or 1 tablespoon*
*   dried mint leaves,*
*   crumbled*

1 tablespoon minced garlic
½ cup olive oil

Use half of the lemon to rub surfaces as you work. Snap back and pull down the leaves and discard, working around the artichoke until the pale yellow leaves are exposed. Trim away about 2 inches from the top of the artichokes. With a paring knife, cut away the dark green around the base. Cut away the dark green exterior of the stalk until the pale green, tender part is exposed. With a small spoon, dig into center of the artichoke and remove the fuzzy choke, scraping against the heart until it is completely clean. Remove any interior leaves that have prickly tips. Fill a large bowl with water and add the juice of the remaining half lemon. Immerse each finished artichoke in the acidulated water to prevent discoloration.

Drain the artichokes. Salt the interiors. Combine the mint, garlic, and a little of the olive oil in small bowl. Add salt to taste. Put the mixture in the center of each artichoke, dividing it equally. Arrange the artichokes stem-side up in a pot just large enough to contain them. Lightly salt them and drizzle with the remaining olive oil. Add enough water to come one-third up to the heart. Bring to a boil. Lower the heat to medium and cover with a tight-fitting lid. Cook until tender but firm; the tip of a knife should slide into the artichoke heart with just the slightest resistance. The time will vary greatly depending on size. Remove the artichokes from the pot with a slotted spoon to a platter. Bring the remaining liquid to a boil and reduce slightly, if necessary. The liquid should be syrupy. Pour the liquid over the artichokes. These can be made up to 2 days in advance but are best when served the same day they are cooked. *Serves 4.*

ARTICHOKES IN TOMATO SAUCE

The artichoke numbers among our favorite vegetables. Here creamy, yellow-green artichoke wedges are simmered in a light tomato sauce. This can be made a day or two in advance. Cleaning artichokes may seem a chore at first, but with a little practice the whole process goes quickly.

6 medium artichokes

2 lemons, halved

1 medium onion, peeled and coarsely chopped

3 tablespoons olive oil

1 large garlic clove, peeled and minced

1 can (28 ounces) peeled Italian tomatoes

Coarse salt to taste

Dash cayenne

Freshly ground pepper

Coarsely chopped fresh flat-leaf parsley and pitted black oil-cured olives for garnish

Completely clean the artichokes of any tough, inedible parts as in Artichokes Roman-Style (see page 138). Cut each cleaned artichoke into 8 wedges, and cut out the choke from each wedge. As you work, rub cut portions with half a lemon. Submerge cleaned artichoke wedges in a large bowl of water containing the juice of half a lemon. Sauté the onion in the olive oil in a large saucepan over low heat until limp. Add the garlic and sauté very briefly. Add the tomatoes and simmer for a few minutes over medium heat. Drain the artichokes and add to the tomato sauce. Add salt and a generous dash of cayenne. Adjust the heat to a gentle simmer and cook, partially covered, for about 45 minutes or until the artichokes are tender when pierced with the tip of a knife. Stir occasionally. If the mixture starts to stick to the pan, add water. Remove pan from heat and add the juice of 1 lemon. If refrigerated, bring to room temperature before serving. Adjust the seasoning. Grind fresh pepper over the artichokes and sprinkle with parsley and olives. *Serves 6 to 8.*

SIMPLE ASPARAGUS

We are fortunate in America to have such a delicious plant so widely cultivated. Asparagus begins to arrive in our markets at the beginning of Spring in a variety of sizes, ranging from the very thin *spaghetti* asparagus to meaty stalks as thick as two fingers. Asparagus should be displayed in the market with the stalks on dampened paper or standing upright in a small amount of water. Look for firm stalks with no trace of dryness or wrinkling. The tips should be compact. We prefer to use the thin varieties in salads (see page 61), frittatas, and as a plate garnish. Thick asparagus should be savored simply drizzled with olive oil and lemon juice, dressed with a Simple Virgin Dressing (see page 263), or dipped into Mimosa Sauce (see page 268). Few dishes are more satisfying eaten with the fingers than a plate of thick asparagus cooked just until tender. Combine asparagus with dressings immediately before serving to prevent discoloration.

2 pounds asparagus

FOR THIN ASPARAGUS:

Make uniform in size by trimming off the tough lower stalks.

FOR THICK ASPARAGUS:

Snap off the tough lower stems. The stalk will usually snap off at the point at which it is no longer tough. Check to be sure. If the stalk still seems fibrous, keep trimming until you arrive at the tender, moist part of the stem. If the skin of the asparagus seems very tough, peel the stalks with a vegetable peeler from about 2 inches below the tips to the end of the stalk.

CONTINUED

TO COOK ALL ASPARAGUS:

Using kitchen twine, tie the asparagus into a bundle, one tie just below the tips and another 2 inches from the bottom. Blanch the bundled asparagus in an abundant amount of boiling water in a large pot for 5 to 7 minutes or until the spears are tender yet firm to the bite. Plunge them immediately into a large bowl filled with ice and water and untie. When the asparagus feel cool to the touch, remove from the water and drain. The asparagus may be cooked the day before serving. Refrigerate covered with a damp (*not wet*) cloth. *Serves 6 to 8.*

ASPARAGUS WITH TOMATOES AND PINE NUTS

The bright ribbon of tomatoes makes a pretty presentation.

2 pounds thin asparagus
2 tomatoes, peeled, seeded,
    and diced fine
1 shallot, peeled and minced
    fine

2 tablespoons pine nuts
Simple Virgin Dressing made
    with 2 tablespoons
    roughly chopped basil (see
    page 263)

Cook the asparagus according to the directions above. Combine the tomatoes, shallot, and pine nuts in a small bowl and moisten with a bit of the Simple Virgin Dressing. Arrange the asparagus on a serving platter. Spoon the tomato mixture across the center of the asparagus in a stripe. Just before serving, drench the asparagus with the Simple Virgin Dressing. Vinegar discolors asparagus, so wait until the last minute to dress them. *Serves 6 to 8 as a first course.*

WHITE BEANS WITH SAGE

This dish is served at the most elegant Florentine restaurants. Americans tend to scorn the bean, considering it a lowly budget-stretcher. That it is economical cannot be denied, but served as a side dish with a tablespoon of fine extra-virgin olive oil, White Beans with Sage often outclasses the accompanying entrée. The elegance of the dish, however, rests in its whole-bean presentation. Overcooked, or cooked too rapidly, the beans can split and become mushy and unappealing. They should be cooked slowly over very low heat so that they do not move with the movement of the water. Cooked this way just until tender, each bean remains separate and whole.

1 pound dry small white, or
*   Great Northern beans*
2½ quarts water
1 large garlic clove, peeled
1 handful fresh sage leaves, or
*   1 teaspoon dried sage*
*   leaves, crumbled*

Coarse salt and freshly ground
*   pepper to taste*
Fruity olive oil

Place the beans, water, garlic, sage, and salt in a heavy cooking pot, preferably earthenware. Cover and place on heat so low that it will take almost an hour for the water to boil. Once the liquid comes to a boil, regulate the heat so that the liquid barely simmers. The beans must not move around during the cooking as it will cause them to break up. If the water level drops greatly, carefully add boiling water. The length of time it takes for the beans to cook depends on their age, but count on at least 3 hours. The beans should retain their shape but be tender to the bite. Cool to room temperature and serve as a side dish. Season to taste. Have fruity olive oil on the table to drizzle on top. *Serves 6 to 8.*

BROCCOLI IN LEMON AND RED CHILE PEPPER

Broccoli, with its clean, strong flavor and electric green color, simply radiates health. Seasoned with lemon and red chile pepper, this wildly flavorful dish deserves to be served as a separate course to be properly relished.

¼ cup olive oil
1 fresh small red chile pepper,
   seeds removed, finely
   chopped, or ½ teaspoon
   crushed dried red chile
   pepper
3 canned flat anchovy fillets

1 bunch broccoli, about 1½
   pounds
Coarse salt
Juice of half a lemon, about 2
   tablespoons
Freshly ground pepper to taste

To make the dressing, put the olive oil, chile pepper, and anchovies in a small sauté pan. Heat the oil until it is just warm and the anchovies melt. Turn off the heat and set aside until needed. Trim the tough ends of the broccoli. Peel the stalks with a paring knife.

Separate the broccoli flowerets into generous pieces. Cut the stalks into a julienne about the same size as the flowerets. Cook the broccoli in boiling salted water to cover in a pot until bright green and tender but crisp, about 10 minutes. Drain and refresh under cold running water. Dry well on paper towels. Place the broccoli in a rustic serving bowl. Dress with the cooled, flavored oil and the lemon juice. Toss gently and season with salt and freshly ground pepper. *Serves 4.*

CAULIFLOWER IN SALSA VERDE

The green color and piquant flavor of the Green Sauce enlivens the cauliflower. It is so tasty that we often serve cauliflower this way as an appetizer with toothpicks. Cooked so the cauliflower is still crunchy, the dish can substitute for a salad course as well.

2 heads cauliflower   *1 recipe Salsa Verde (see page 269)*

Cut the cauliflower in half. Cut out and discard the woody core with a sharp knife. Break the cauliflower into flowerets. Cook in an abundant amount of boiling salted water just until tender. The cauliflower should still have a snap to it. Drain in a colander and rinse under cold running water until it feels cool to the touch. Drain thoroughly. Toss in a bowl with the Salsa Verde. Allow to marinate in the refrigerator for at least 1 hour. This can be made up to 2 days ahead. Toss before serving. *Serves 6 to 8 as accompanying vegetable, 4 to 6 as a salad.*

CAPONATA DELLA NONNA
grandmother's eggplant

In Palermo, caponata is served as an appetizer or spread on crostini. It may also be used in sandwiches or served as a vegetable side dish. Refrigerated, caponata lasts for a week. Its characteristic sweet and sour flavor is quite pronounced in our version.

*2 eggplants, cut into 1-inch
    cubes*
Coarse salt
1 cup vegetable oil
2 tablespoons olive oil
1 cup chopped onion
4 tablespoons tomato paste
*2 cups celery hearts, cut
    crosswise into ½-inch
    slices*

*1 cup green olives, pitted and
    coarsely chopped*
*1 small jar capers, about 3½
    ounces*
6 tablespoons sugar
½ cup red wine vinegar

Sprinkle the eggplant cubes in a colander with salt. Drain for about 1 hour. Shake the colander to remove the water. Pat the eggplant cubes dry with paper towels. Pour vegetable oil into a large skillet to a depth of ¼ to ½ inch. Heat the oil and fry the eggplant in small batches, adding vegetable oil as needed. Remove the cooked eggplant from the skillet with a slotted spoon and place on paper towels to drain. Discard the vegetable oil from the skillet and add the olive oil. Sauté the chopped onion over medium heat. Add the tomato paste and cook until thickened.

Meanwhile, cook the celery in 1 cup of boiling water in a small saucepan until crisp tender. To the onion–tomato paste mixture, add the celery and its cooking liquid, the olives, and capers. Add salt to taste. Simmer the sauce for 5 minutes. Add the eggplant, sugar, and red wine vinegar. Simmer for 5 minutes. Cool to room temperature. Refrigerate up to 1 week. *Serves 6 as a side dish.*

M A R I N A T E D   E G G P L A N T

Every time we serve these rich, deep tasting, aromatic slices of eggplant, we regret not making twice as much. It is one of our favorite ways of preparing eggplant. To use Japanese eggplant when in season: Cut each one lengthwise into quarters, place in a roasting pan, drizzle with olive oil, and bake at 400° until browned. In addition, the Japanese eggplant or eggplant slices can be cooked on a grill. The grilled flavor is marvelous, and grilling uses less oil.

1 eggplant
Coarse salt
Olive oil for frying
1 bunch fresh basil leaves,
*   coarsely chopped, or 1*
*   tablespoon dried basil*
*   leaves, crumbled*

3 garlic cloves, peeled and
*   finely chopped*
¼ cup red wine vinegar

Cut a slice off the stem and blossom ends of the eggplant. Cut lengthwise into thin slices, about ¼ inch thick. Lay out the eggplant slices on paper towels and salt generously. Let stand until beads of water appear on the surface. Dry the eggplant with additional paper towels. Heat a non-stick skillet over high heat. Pour enough oil into the skillet to just cover the bottom. Fry the eggplant slices at moderately high heat a few at a time to avoid crowding in the pan. The slices should brown quickly so that they do not get mushy. As the slices brown, remove them from the pan and place on paper towels to drain.

In a glass or enamel baking dish, make a layer of eggplant slices. Sprinkle some of the basil, garlic, and vinegar over the eggplant slices. Make another layer of eggplant slices, and repeat sprinkling with herbs and vinegar. Continue until all the eggplant is layered and topped with herbs and vinegar. Refrigerate, covered with plastic wrap, for several hours, preferably overnight. The marinated eggplant will continue to improve in flavor for several days. *Serves 4.*

HERB-STUFFED EGGPLANT

The mild flavor of eggplant is a good vehicle for herbs. Once cooked the eggplant is creamy inside and beautifully browned on the outside. Red or white wine can be used in the recipe. When preparing for a crowd, place the stuffed eggplants into a roasting pan, drizzle olive oil on top, and roast at 400° until browned.

3–4 Japanese eggplants, or 2–
    3 very small eggplants
Coarse salt
3 tablespoons olive oil

1½ cups chopped fresh herbs
    of your choice (basil,
    parsley, oregano, mint,
    marjoram), or ½ cup
    dried herbs (oregano,
    basil, mint, marjoram), or
    a mixture of fresh and
    dried herbs
¼ cup wine or water

Cut each Japanese eggplant in half lengthwise, but do not remove the stem. If regular eggplants are very round, cut them lengthwise into quarters. Score the eggplants by making diagonal, shallow slashes into the flesh. Salt the eggplants generously and let them sit for 20 minutes so that the water comes to the surface. Blot the eggplants dry with paper towels. While holding the eggplant so that the slashes open slightly, push approximately 2 tablespoons of herb mixture into each slash.

Heat the olive oil in a large skillet. When the oil is hot, place the eggplant halves cut-side down in the oil. Fry for 5 minutes over high heat. Pour the wine or water over the eggplant, cover, lower the heat, and braise for 5 to 10 more minutes or until the eggplants are tender. Remove the cover. If any liquid remains, turn up the heat and cook until it evaporates. Remove the eggplants to a platter. Cool and serve at room temperature. *Serves 4 to 6.*

ESCALIVADA
grilled mixed vegetables

Escalivada, though Catalan, is completely in keeping with Italian culinary tradition and the technique for grilling vegetables in both countries is identical. This recipe comes from chef Montse Guillen of El Internacionale in New York City. It is an ideal dish for a summer beach picnic or for a backyard barbecue. Use a wood charcoal like mesquite or hickory, not a petroleum product. Making this dish can provide group entertainment for an afternoon and restore some of the ritual surrounding eating. Cooking over an open fire is an important one. Escalivada is served as an entrée. The recipe follows in Montse Guillen's words.

2 Spanish onions, unpeeled
2 large green bell peppers
2 large red bell peppers
2 eggplants
6 tomatoes

Coarse salt
4 tablespoons olive oil
6 garlic cloves, peeled and
    minced

Make a wood fire and when it dies down, place the vegetables directly on the embers. The onions cook much more slowly than the other vegetables, about 1 hour, so put them on the fire first. Turn the vegetables from time to time until the skin is well burned. When you judge that they are cooked, remove them from the fire and scrape away the charred skin. Cut up the peppers and eggplants lengthwise. Cut the onions lengthwise into quarters. Put these vegetables on a platter, salt, and anoint them with plenty of olive oil and a little minced garlic. The tomatoes should be served separately. *Serves 4 to 6.*

Greens

The slightly acerbic flavor of cooked greens is pleasing and welcome, a flavor we associate with their cleansing, health-giving properties. They are extremely rich in vitamins and minerals and are available all year long in one variety or another. A platter with a mound of freshly cooked spinach is a beautiful sight, dark green, glossy, and inviting.

We include four recipes for different greens but they can easily be adapted to others available to you. They are all good as part of a light lunch or dinner, or as a component in a more elaborate buffet.

Remember that greens cook down dramatically. When increasing a recipe, make sure you buy enough even though the amount, uncooked, may strike you as somewhat extreme. Wash greens well in several changes of water. Cook greens only long enough to remove all traces of rawness or crunchiness. Overcooking undermines flavor and texture. Greens should be served at room temperature and, ideally, once cooked, they should never be refrigerated for they lose their fresh flavor. Any remaining flavorful cooking liquid can be drunk. Not only does it have a brisk and bracing flavor, but it is considered a restorative. At one time in Italy, there were white-tiled bars lined with stools where a variety of greens, mostly wild, sometimes very bitter, were boiled in large cauldrons. People would patronize these *Erbaioli* early in the morning to buy the cooking water which was sold as a hot drink possessing beneficial properties meant to cure a variety of ailments. Each green contained specific healing properties.

BRAISED ESCAROLE WITH CELERY

The celery lends a fresh, clean taste to this simple savory dish.

1 head escarole, washed
3 tablespoons olive oil
1 garlic clove, peeled and
  minced
3 celery stalks, peeled and cut
  into ½-inch diagonal pieces

¼ cup water
Coarse salt and freshly ground
  pepper to taste
1 lemon

Cut the escarole leaves into strips 1 to 2 inches wide. Heat 2 tablespoons of the olive oil in a medium skillet. Add the garlic, celery, and escarole. Stir over high heat until the escarole wilts slightly. Add the water. Cover the skillet and cook over low heat 10 minutes or until the celery is just tender. Remove the cover. Add the salt and pepper to taste, raise the heat, and cook until almost all the liquid evaporates. Turn the mixture out into a serving dish and cool to room temperature. Before serving, drizzle the remaining olive oil and squeeze lemon juice over the escarole. *Serves 4 as a side dish.*

KALE AND BLACK OLIVES

Kale has an aggressive, somewhat bitter flavor that we enjoy. The black olives match the strong tasting vegetable in intensity. If desired, the greens can be surrounded with quartered hard-cooked eggs which act as a flavor foil and lend a mellowing presence.

2 pounds kale

4 tablespoons olive oil

2 garlic cloves, peeled and
    minced

¾ cup black oil-cured olives,
    pitted and coarsely
    chopped

Coarse salt to taste

Lemon wedges

Hard-cooked eggs (optional)

Strip the leaves off the stems of kale, and tear the leaves into 2 or 3 pieces. Discard any yellowed leaves. Wash well in several changes of cold water. Cook, uncovered, in an abundant amount of boiling salted water in a large pot just until tender, about 20 minutes. Drain and press out excess water with a fork. Heat the olive oil with the garlic and olives in a sauté pan over low heat. Add the kale and sauté for a few minutes. The olives will impart flavor and saltiness to the greens, so adjust the salt toward the end of the cooking. Mound the kale on a platter. Garnish with lemon wedges or optional hard-cooked eggs. Serve at room temperature. *Serves 4 to 6.*

SPINACH WITH ANCHOVIES

Since many people say they hate anchovies, we stopped mentioning them as an ingredient in this dish, and no one has ever guessed. Anchovies are splendid for salting certain dishes; they give a great additional punch.

2 pounds spinach, washed
2–3 tablespoons olive oil
4 garlic cloves, peeled and
coarsely chopped

2 canned flat anchovy fillets,
finely chopped
Coarse salt and freshly ground
pepper to taste

Cut off any long, tough stems from the spinach. Heat the oil in a skillet and add the garlic and anchovy. Stir over low heat until the anchovy begins to dissolve. Add the spinach and turn heat up to medium. Add the salt and pepper, if necessary. Lightly sauté just until the spinach wilts. Do not overcook. The spinach should be glossy and bright green in color. Serve at room temperature. *Serves 4 to 6.*

SWISS CHARD WITH LEMON

Swiss chard has a mild, sweet taste that is best left alone with only a squeeze of lemon juice to bring out the flavor. The lemon juice is added at the last moment so the Swiss chard does not discolor. Look for young Swiss chard with small stalks. Red chard is occasionally available and can be prepared in the same way. If possible, do not refrigerate chard before serving because it detracts from the flavor even when brought back to room temperature. The stalks can be diced and used in Summer Minestrone with Pesto (page 35).

2 pounds Swiss chard
Coarse salt to taste
2–3 tablespoons fruity olive
oil

Lemon wedges

Strip the green leaves from the stalks. Discard any bruised or wilted areas on the leaves. Wash the chard leaves in several changes of water until no trace of sand or dirt remains. Put in a large pot with only the water that clings to the leaves. Add salt. Cover and cook over medium heat until tender, about 10 minutes. Turn into a colander and let drain. Press out the remaining moisture with the back of a spoon. Let cool. Before serving, moisten with the olive oil and add salt to taste. Garnish with lemon wedges. *Serves 4.*

VERDURE AL FORNO
baked vegetable gratin

Good picnic food. Best if baked in an earthenware dish.

6 medium zucchini, about 1
    pound
Coarse salt
1 pound spinach, washed
1 medium onion, peeled and
    chopped
5 tablespoons olive oil and a
    little for oiling the baking
    dish
3 garlic cloves, peeled and
    minced

½ cup grated Parmesan
    cheese and 2 tablespoons
    for topping
2 eggs, lightly beaten
2 tablespoons chopped fresh
    parsley or fresh basil
    leaves
1 cup cooked garbanzo beans
Freshly ground pepper to taste

Cut the zucchini into ½-inch dice. Place in a colander, salt, and drain for 20 minutes. Cut off any long stems from the spinach. Cook the spinach with the water that clings to the leaves in a pot, along with a little salt just until the spinach wilts. Drain and let cool. Squeeze out the excess water and coarsely chop. Gently sauté the onion in 3 tablespoons of the olive oil in a skillet over low heat for 20 minutes or until the onion is soft and pale gold.

Meanwhile, pat the zucchini dry with paper towels. Add to the onion and sauté for 10 minutes. Add the spinach and garlic and sauté for an additional 2 to 3 minutes. Turn into a bowl and let cool. Combine the vegetables with the Parmesan, eggs, parsley or basil, garbanzo beans, salt, and pepper. Lightly oil a shallow, round baking dish. Fill the baking dish with the spinach mixture. Sprinkle the top with 2 tablespoons grated Parmesan and drizzle with the 2 tablespoons olive oil. Bake in a preheated 375° oven for 45 minutes to 1 hour or until a golden crust has formed. Let cool. Serve at room temperature. *Serves 6.*

SWEET AND SOUR LEEKS

Although any simple preparation of leeks such as a vinaigrette leads to an elegant presentation, we enjoy the unusual, robust flavor of this version.

2 bunches leeks, or 3 bunches
    baby leeks
2 tablespoons pine nuts
¼ cup olive oil
1 tablespoon currants

3 medium tomatoes, peeled,
    seeded and chopped
    coarsely
¼ cup vinegar
2 tablespoons brown sugar
Coarse salt to taste

Trim the leeks of the green tops, leaving only 1 or 2 inches of pale green. Clean the leeks thoroughly of sand and dirt by making a lengthwise slit through the top of the leek and down halfway into the white; rinse well under cold running water. Sauté the pine nuts in 2 tablespoons of the olive oil in a large sauteuse or sauté pan with high sides over low heat. When they begin to color, add the currants and tomatoes. Sauté the mixture over moderate heat for a few minutes or until the tomatoes begin to break down and become saucy. Add the trimmed and cleaned leeks to the pan. Add the remaining olive oil and enough water to come halfway up the sides of the leeks. Bring the liquid to a simmer, partially cover the pan, and braise the leeks for about 15 minutes or until they are tender when pierced with a knife. Remove the leeks gently from the pan, and place them on a serving platter or in a glass or enamel dish. Turn the heat to high and begin to reduce the remaining pan juices. Add the vinegar and sugar to the pan, tasting for sweet and sour, adjusting to your taste by adding more sugar or vinegar if you wish. Add salt. Continue to reduce the pan juices until the sauce has body. Pour the hot sauce over the leeks. Let cool and serve at room temperature. *Serves 4 to 6 as a first course.*

MUSHROOMS WITH MINT AND TOMATO

These create a quantity of delectable juices, so serve with plenty of good bread. They last for a week refrigerated and, in fact, intensify in flavor. Bring to room temperature before serving.

1 pound medium mushrooms
6 tablespoons olive oil
2 large garlic cloves, peeled
and thinly sliced
1 large tomato, roasted,
peeled, seeded, and diced
3 tablespoons lemon juice
2 teaspoons red wine vinegar

1 tablespoon minced fresh
mint leaves, or 1 teaspoon
dried mint leaves,
crumbled
Dash cayenne
Coarse salt and freshly ground
pepper to taste

Clean the mushrooms by wiping them with a damp cloth or paper towels. Trim the stems. Heat the olive oil in a sauté pan. Add the mushrooms and garlic and toss in the oil. Cover and cook over medium heat for 2 to 4 minutes or until a mushroom cut in half is barely cooked at the center. Add the tomato and cook for another minute. Off the heat, add the lemon juice, vinegar, mint, cayenne, and plenty of salt and freshly ground pepper. Put in a rustic serving dish and let cool. *Serves 4.*

GRILLED STUFFED WILD MUSHROOMS

These mushrooms are best grilled, preferably over mesquite charcoal. The grilling combines the fresh thyme and the deep flavor of the mushrooms to produce an intense, woodsy flavor. The mushrooms are a perfect complement to grilled meats and game, or as an appetizer eaten with a handful of olives.

15 large shiitake mushrooms,
*   or large brown mushrooms*
2 bunches fresh thyme leaves
6–8 garlic cloves, peeled and
*   finely chopped*

Coarse salt to taste
¼ cup fruity olive oil

Clean the mushrooms with a damp towel. Trim off the woody stems. Remove the thyme leaves from the stems and chop fine. Mix together the chopped thyme, garlic, and salt, at least two teaspoons, in a small bowl. Make shallow slits in the thickest part of the mushroom cap. Stuff the herb mixture into the slits and into the gills on the underside of the cap. Brush the mushrooms with the olive oil. Place on a hot grill, gill-side up, or under a hot broiler until the mushrooms soften slightly, about 3 to 5 minutes. We do not recommend substituting dried thyme for fresh. If fresh thyme is unavailable, use garlic only or substitute another fresh herb of your choice. Serve at room temperature. *Serves 4 to 6 as an appetizer.*

PEARL ONIONS BRAISED IN ORANGE JUICE

The orange juice and olive oil combine with the onions to form a rich-tasting, glossy sauce. Let the onions marinate for a day or longer to allow the flavor of the sauce to penetrate. Refrigerate for up to a week. Serve as a sweet accent to a simple roast chicken or roast pork. Look for firm pearl onions that have not sprouted.

*2 pounds pearl onions of
   similar size, about 28*
*1½ cups orange juice, freshly
   squeezed*
Grated peel of 1 orange
½ cup olive oil

*Coarse salt and freshly ground
   pepper to taste*
*2 tablespoons fresh flat-leaf
   parsley, stemmed and
   roughly chopped*

Bring a large pot of salted water to a boil. Add the onions and cook for 3 to 4 minutes. Drain in a colander and refresh the onions under cold running water. Peel and trim the root end, but leave the root intact or the onions will fall apart. Combine the onions, orange juice, grated peel, olive oil and salt in a saucepan. Cook until the onions are tender yet crisp, testing for doneness with tip of knife. Transfer to a gratin dish and bake in a preheated 400° oven for 10 to 15 minutes or until the onions are soft and golden. Taste for salt. Just before serving, grind pepper over the onions and sprinkle with chopped parsley. Serve at room temperature. *Serves 6.*

ROASTED RED OR YELLOW ONIONS IN BALSAMIC VINEGAR

These rustic, roasted onions have a rich, burnished look. Roasting brings out the sweetness of the onions, especially the red onions. They are easy to make in quantity and therefore great to include on a buffet.

*4 medium red or yellow
    onions, unpeeled
Olive oil*

*Coarse salt and freshly ground
    pepper to taste
¼ cup balsamic vinegar*

Coat the unpeeled onions generously with olive oil. Sprinkle with salt and pepper. Place them in a roasting pan just large enough to hold them. Roast the onions in a preheated 375° oven for 1 hour or longer depending on the size of the onions. They should be soft to the touch. Remove the onions from the pan and let cool slightly. Cut in half through the root end and arrange on a platter, cut-side up. To deglaze the roasting pan, add the vinegar and place the pan over medium heat. Boil the vinegar for a few minutes, scraping the caramelized onion juices off the bottom of the pan. Reduce the liquid until it is syrupy and dark, glossy brown. Spoon a little of the thickened liquid over the onions, completely coating the cut surfaces. Let them cool. *Serves 6 to 8.*

FRIED PEPPERS

These peppers never fail to be received with outright astonishment. Guests are amazed that so simple a preparation yields such tasty results. Whenever we make this dish, we think of a friend frying peppers over a propane stove in an unfinished country house in Tuscany. The longer the peppers cook without becoming dark brown or burned at the edges, the sweeter they will be. Red or yellow bell peppers work best in this recipe. We do not recommend using only green ones for they are not sweet enough. If you decide to make the peppers in advance, remember to let them come to room temperature before serving so that the oil will liquify.

4 bell peppers, preferably of   *Olive oil*
    assorted colors

Stem and seed the peppers and cut into vertical slices ½ inch wide, trimming away the thick white ribs. Heat enough olive oil in a medium heavy skillet to cover the bottom of the pan. When the oil is hot, add the sliced peppers. Turn the heat to moderate and cook the peppers until soft with a few browned edges. When done, lift the peppers out of the oil with tongs or a slotted spoon and onto a bowl or platter. Cool to room temperature. Do not serve cold. *Serves 6 to 8.*

MARINATED ROASTED PEPPERS WITH OREGANO

The strong, gutsy flavor of dried oregano works better in this dish than the more subtle flavor of fresh.

6 bell peppers, preferably of   *¼–½ cup fruity olive oil*
    assorted colors   *⅛–¼ cup red wine vinegar*
8 garlic cloves, peeled   *Freshly ground pepper*
1 tablespoon dried oregano
    leaves

Roast and peel the peppers (see page 94). Cut them lengthwise into strips about 1½ inches wide. Layer the pepper strips in a plastic or glass container with the garlic and oregano. Pour olive oil over the peppers and marinate at least 12 hours or overnight. They will keep well for a couple of weeks if kept covered with olive oil. If refrigerated, let come to room temperature so the oil will liquify. Before serving, splash with vinegar and grind pepper over. *Serves 6 to 8.*

RED BELL PEPPERS STUFFED WITH TOMATO AND ANCHOVY

Little work produces a dish with spectacular effect. If yellow peppers are in season, this is the perfect dish to show off their smooth flavor and bright color. You can easily vary the peppers by adding pitted oil-cured black olives and 1 tablespoon of grated mozzarella on top of the tomatoes during the last few minutes of cooking. Either way, this is an excellent buffet dish.

4 red or yellow bell peppers
4 medium tomatoes, coarsely chopped
6 canned flat anchovy fillets

3 tablespoons olive oil
Coarse salt and freshly ground pepper to taste

Cut the peppers in half lengthwise, remove the stems, seeds, and thick ribs or membranes, and arrange cut-side up in a shallow baking dish. Place 1 to 2 tablespoons of chopped tomato in each pepper half and an anchovy fillet on top of the tomatoes. Drizzle 1 teaspoon of olive oil over each pepper half. Season with salt and pepper. Bake in a preheated 375° oven for about 45 minutes or until the peppers have softened. Reserve the juice that has collected in the dish. Cool the peppers and arrange on a serving platter. Moisten with the reserved juices. *Serves 8.*

YELLOW BELL PEPPERS IN VINEGAR, SUGAR, AND OREGANO

We tasted this on the island of Ustica off the coast of Palermo. It was prepared by Mario, the owner and chef of a small restaurant. Featured were grilled local fish of which there is an abundance. The vinegar-sugar combination is a popular one in Italy and is used with many different foods including meats, fish, and vegetables. We especially like it here because of the intense sweetness of the yellow bell peppers. When buying bell peppers, make sure the skin is smooth, not shriveled, and that there are no soft spots on the flesh.

4 yellow bell peppers
3 tablespoons olive oil
2 tablespoons red wine vinegar
1 tablespoon sugar
1 teaspoon dried oregano leaves
Coarse salt to taste

Cut the peppers in half lengthwise and remove the stems, seeds, and membranes. Slice into ¾-inch-wide strips. Cook the bell peppers in the olive oil in a skillet, covered, over low heat for about 8 minutes. Stir occasionally to prevent the peppers from browning. The peppers should have some crunch to them. Add the vinegar, sugar, oregano, and salt and stir. Cook another 2 or 3 minutes. If using dried oregano on the stem, garnish the peppers with some sprigs. Serve at room temperature. *Serves 4.*

SAGE POTATOES

These potatoes are simple to prepare, cooked quickly using this method which combines frying and steaming. Creamy soft inside with a golden crust outside, these potatoes are fragrant with sage. A good accompaniment to simply prepared meats like Arista (see page 220).

4–6 medium russet potatoes, peeled
1 garlic clove, peeled
¼ cup olive oil
3–4 fresh sage leaves, minced, or 1 teaspoon dried sage leaves, crumbled

Coarse salt and freshly ground pepper to taste

Cut the peeled potatoes in half lengthwise and crosswise into 1-inch-wide pieces. If not using the potato pieces immediately, drop them into cold water to prevent browning. Sauté the garlic in the oil in a skillet. Drain and dry the potatoes if they have been in water. Add the potatoes to the pan. Shake to coat the potatoes with the oil. Add the sage, salt, and pepper and cover. Turn the heat to low and let the potatoes steam, tossing them occasionally in the pan. When the potatoes are tender, about 10 to 15 minutes, remove the cover, increase the heat to high, and let the potatoes get a little crusty. Serve tepid. *Serves 4 to 6.*

SPINACH CROQUETTES

4 bunches spinach, washed
Coarse salt
3 eggs
Freshly ground pepper to taste

1 cup homemade bread
crumbs
Oil for frying
Lemon wedges

Cook the spinach in a large pot with just the water that clings to the leaves and a little salt just until wilted. Drain and let cool. Squeeze the excess water out of the spinach. Chop fine. Beat 1 of the eggs. Combine it with the chopped spinach. Season with a generous amount of salt and pepper. Form into 12 equal patties. Beat the remaining 2 eggs in a small bowl. Spread the bread crumbs in a dish. Dip the patties in the bread crumbs, then in the eggs, and once again in the bread crumbs. Heat about 1 inch of oil in a skillet. When the oil is hot, fry the patties 2 or 3 at a time, turning them to brown both sides. Drain on paper towels. Salt the exteriors lightly. Serve at room temperature with lemon wedges. *Serves 4 to 6.*

SUMMER SQUASH STUFFED WITH VEAL RISOTTO

Italian arborio rice has a marvelous capacity for absorbing liquid yet retaining its shape and texture. In this recipe the rice stuffing is creamy and moist. The veal and thyme enrich the flavor, creating a delicious, savory dish.

6–8 pattypan squash, or round
    zucchini if available
1 onion, peeled and minced
1 garlic clove, peeled and
    minced
2 tablespoons butter
1 tablespoon oil
¼ pound ground veal

2–3 fresh thyme sprigs, or 1
    teaspoon dried thyme
    leaves, crumbled
Coarse salt and freshly ground
    pepper to taste
1 cup arborio rice
½ cup heavy cream
1½–2 cups chicken broth

Cut off the stem end from each squash in one thin slice and reserve. With a melon baller, scoop out the squash, being careful not to cut into the skin; the shells should be intact. Reserve the insides of the squash. Drop the squash shells and tops into an abundant amount of boiling salted water in a large pot. Blanch briefly, 1 to 2 minutes, and refresh under cold running water. Drain in a colander and then on paper towels.

Meanwhile, to make the filling, coarsely chop the reserved squash balls. Sauté the squash, onion, and garlic in the butter and oil in a medium skillet over low heat until the squash is tender. Add the ground veal, stirring to break up the meat. Add the thyme, salt, and pepper and sauté until veal is nearly cooked. Add the rice to the skillet. Sauté the rice with the meat and squash mixture until the grains glisten and become slightly opaque, 2 to 3 minutes. Add the cream and stir over low heat until all of the liquid is absorbed. Add 1½ cups of the chicken broth, stir, and cover the skillet. Cook over low heat until the liquid is absorbed. Check frequently, adding more broth if necessary. The rice when done should be tender yet slightly resistant to the bite. Taste the mixture for seasoning. When the rice is cooked, let cool to room temperature. Remove the thyme sprigs. CONTINUED

Generously stuff each squash shell with the rice mixture. Set the stem slice atop each squash. Serve as a vegetable accompaniment or as a component in an antipasto. *Serves 4 to 6.*

S W E E T   A N D   S O U R   S Q U A S H

A specialty of Palermo prepared often by Viana's family. The combination of red squash and mint with vinegar is a unique juxtaposition of flavors that never fails to delight.

1 pound banana squash
Olive oil for frying
¾ cup red wine vinegar, or
*   balsamic vinegar*
¼ cup tightly packed fresh
*   mint leaves, coarsely*
*   chopped, or 1 tablespoon*
*   dried mint leaves,*
*   crumbled*

2 teaspoons sugar
1 small garlic clove, peeled
*   and minced (optional)*
Fresh mint leaves for garnish

Peel the squash with a vegetable peeler. Cut the squash lengthwise in half and then crosswise into ¼-inch-thick slices. Pour oil into a heavy skillet to a depth of ¼ inch. Heat the oil and add the half moons of squash. Fry one layer at a time without crowding the pan, until each slice is golden brown, turning once. The squash should be tender but still hold its shape, with a pattern of golden brown dots. As the slices brown, remove them with tongs or a fork to drain on paper towels.

When all the squash is cooked, blot the pieces of excess oil and arrange in a shallow glass or enamel baking dish. Pour off the remaining oil from skillet. Add the vinegar, mint leaves, sugar, and garlic, if desired. Bring the vinegar to a boil. Lower the heat and simmer until the vinegar has reduced slightly. Pour the hot liquid over the squash. Refrigerate and let marinate for several hours or overnight. This can be done up to 2 days ahead. To serve, lift the squash out of the marinade with tongs or a slotted spoon and arrange the slices on a platter. Garnish with fresh mint leaves. *Serves 4 as a vegetable side dish.*

T O M A T O   G R A T I N

6 large firm tomatoes
3 tablespoons fruity olive oil
¼ cup coarsely chopped fresh
    oregano leaves, or 1
    tablespoon dried oregano
    leaves, crumbled

2 tablespoons capers
Coarse salt and freshly ground
    pepper to taste
¼ cup bread crumbs

Core the tomatoes and cut crosswise into thick slices. Grease a large gratin dish with 1 tablespoon of the olive oil. Spread half of the tomato slices on the bottom of the dish. Sprinkle with the oregano and half the capers and season with salt and pepper. Arrange the remaining tomatoes on top. Sprinkle with the rest of the capers and top with the bread crumbs. Season with salt and pepper and drizzle with olive oil. Bake for 20 minutes in a preheated 450° oven or until the bread crumbs are golden brown. Let cool completely. Serve chilled or at room temperature. *Serves 4 to 6.*

HERB-STUFFED TOMATOES

This simple tomato preparation is beautiful, fresh tasting, and easy to make and serve for large crowds.

¼ cup minced fresh parsley
  leaves
3–5 large fresh basil leaves,
  minced
1 garlic clove, peeled and
  minced

1 teaspoon coarse salt
4 firm ripe tomatoes, halved
  and seeded
Fruity olive oil

Mix together the parsley, basil, garlic, and salt in a small bowl. Stuff the tomato cavities loosely with the herb mixture. Place the stuffed tomato halves in a small roasting pan. Drizzle olive oil lightly on top of the tomatoes. Bake in a preheated 375° oven for about 10 to 15 minutes or until the tomatoes have softened but still hold their shape. Serve at room temperature. *Serves 6 to 8.*

RICE-STUFFED TOMATOES

The addition of mint leaves gives these traditional Italian tomatoes an added brightness when served cold or at room temperature. Although most traditional recipes call for stuffing the tomatoes with raw rice, we find that the long cooking often results in an unappealing mushy tomato. We therefore recommend partially precooking the rice. Garnish with fresh mint leaves. Delicious with thinly sliced cold steak.

6 large tomatoes

⅓ cup long-grain white rice

3–4 fresh basil leaves, minced

2 teaspoons minced fresh mint
   leaves

2 teaspoons minced fresh
   parsley leaves

1 small garlic clove, peeled
   and minced

Coarse salt to taste

Fruity olive oil

Cut a ½-inch slice off the top of the tomatoes at the stem end. Reserve the tops. Remove the seeds from the cavities into a bowl. Drain the tomatoes in a sieve over the same bowl. When all the tomatoes have been emptied of seeds and excess liquid, strain the liquid from seeds. Discard the seeds and save the resulting tomato juice. Cook the rice in an abundant amount of boiling salted water for 7 to 10 minutes or until the rice is about two-thirds cooked. It should still have a definite bite to it. Drain the rice in a sieve and refresh under cold running water. Drain. Mix together in a small bowl the rice, the minced herbs, garlic, and salt. Stuff the tomato cavities with the rice mixture so that the cavities are almost filled. Place the tomatoes in a small baking dish just large enough to hold them. Drizzle 1 spoonful of the reserved tomato juice over each tomato. Drizzle about 1 teaspoon olive oil on each tomato. Place the reserved tops on the stuffed tomatoes like lids. Pour the remaining reserved tomato juices in the pan around the tomatoes to a depth of approximately ½ inch. Add water if necessary. Bake the tomatoes in a preheated 375° oven for about 15 minutes or until the rice is completely cooked and the tomatoes have slightly softened without losing their shape. Serve at room temperature. *Serves 6.*

TOMATO HALVES WITH PARSLEY SAUCE

A piquant counterpoint to meat and fish, especially fine served with Pollo Tonnato (see page 230). Use flat-leaf parsley if available. Parsley is an herb that is so commonly available it is taken for granted. It has a fresh, bracing flavor that should be appreciated more than just as an extraneous garnish. In this dish it predominates.

½ cup finely minced fresh flat-leaf parsley leaves

1 garlic clove, peeled and minced

4 canned flat anchovy fillets, minced

¼ cup fruity olive oil

2 tablespoons lemon juice

Coarse salt and freshly ground pepper to taste

4 firm ripe tomatoes, halved and seeded

Combine the parsley, garlic, anchovy, olive oil, lemon juice, salt, and pepper in a small bowl. Lightly salt the interior of the tomatoes. Spoon some of the sauce into each tomato half. Serve at room temperature. *Serves 4.*

WHOLE ROASTED TOMATOES WITH BASIL-FLAVORED OLIVE OIL

The success of this simple dish rests on the use of highly flavored olive oil and red, ripe tomatoes. On page 262 we give instructions for making flavored oils. We recommend using either basil or oregano. If you want to make just enough flavored oil to use in this recipe, combine the basil and oil a week ahead, using the amounts in this recipe. Keep in the refrigerator.

6 firm ripe tomatoes
Coarse salt and freshly ground
    pepper to taste
6 fresh basil leaves

½ cup basil-flavored olive oil
    or 1 cup fruity olive oil
    and 1 large bunch fresh
basil

Spear the stem end of a tomato on a meat fork and carefully roast over a gas flame or under a hot broiler, turning frequently until the skin cracks slightly and the tomato is lightly charred in one or two spots. Repeat with the other tomatoes. Peel. Cut out the core of each, making an opening approximately 1½ inches in diameter. Gently cut into each cavity and remove some, but not all, of the tomato seeds. Press down lightly on the tomato to flatten the bottom so that it stands upright. Salt the inside of each tomato. Place a basil leaf in each tomato, spoon 2 tablespoons flavored oil into each, and grind pepper over the tomatoes. This dish can be made hours in advance. Serve at room temperature. *Serves 6.*

GRILLED GREEN OR GOLDEN ZUCCHINI

Grilling adds an amazing depth and richness to the flavor of zucchini, with the mellowed presence of basil and garlic adding further dimension.

6 medium zucchini
Coarse salt
¼ cup olive oil
5 large fresh basil leaves

3 garlic cloves, peeled and
*   slivered*
Freshly ground pepper to taste

Trim the ends of the zucchini. Cut lengthwise into slices approximately ⅜ inch thick. Salt the slices and let drain on paper towels for 30 minutes. Wipe dry. Arrange the slices on a baking sheet. Brush lightly with olive oil. Place under a preheated broiler close to the source of heat. Grill on both sides until the zucchini are golden brown, basting with olive oil as they cook. The zucchini can also be cooked on an outdoor grill by placing them directly on the grill. Layer the cooked zucchini in a wide, shallow serving dish. Tear the basil leaves and scatter with the slivered garlic over each layer. Season with salt and pepper and moisten with olive oil. Cover with plastic wrap and refrigerate overnight. Bring to room temperature before serving. *Serves 4 to 6.*

ZUCCHINI IN CARPIONE WITH MINT

zucchini marinated in vinegar and mint

Cooking *in carpione* is a way of preserving foods in vinegar. Vinegar and mint give this golden fried zucchini a clean, refreshing quality. It mellows as it marinates, softening the sharp vinegar edge. This can be refrigerated for several days.

6 medium zucchini
½ cup olive oil
2 garlic cloves, peeled and minced
2 tablespoons coarsely chopped fresh mint leaves

Coarse salt and freshly ground pepper to taste
½ cup wine vinegar

Cut the zucchini lengthwise into ¼-inch-thick slices. Heat the oil in a skillet. Fry the zucchini, one layer at a time, until both sides are golden. Remove the slices with a slotted spoon, allowing the oil from the slices to drain back into the pan before transfering to a serving dish. Combine the garlic and mint in a small bowl. Sprinkle over the zucchini. Season with salt and pepper. Bring the vinegar to a boil in a small saucepan. Pour over the zucchini. Let cool. Cover and marinate in the refrigerator at least overnight. *Serves 6.*

f i s h   a n d   s e a f o o d

S A L M O N E   C R U D O
m a r i n a t e d   r a w   s a l m o n   w i t h   b a s i l

N o dish is more simple or more simply elegant. Lovely with drinks or champagne at a small cocktail party. Do not make more than one hour in advance.

*1 pound salmon fillets, skin
    removed*
Juice of 2 lemons
Juice of 2 limes

1 tablespoon olive oil
3 teaspoons minced fresh basil
Freshly ground pepper to taste

CONTINUED

Remove the pin bones from the salmon, using a pliers or your fingers. Using a sharp, thin knife, cut the salmon into paper-thin, diagonal pieces. Place the salmon pieces in a single layer in a glass or enamel dish. Spoon the lemon and lime juices over the salmon. Let the salmon marinate in the citrus juices until it "cooks." The red flesh of the salmon will turn pink and become opaque in about 2 minutes or so. Refrigerate until ready to serve. To serve, lift the salmon pieces out of the juices and arrange decoratively on a serving plate. Drizzle the olive oil over the salmon, rubbing it into the fish. Sprinkle the minced basil over the fish and grind pepper over to taste. Serve as an appetizer with black bread or rye crackers, or as a first course. *Serves 8 to 10 as an appetizer.*

GRAVLAX ALL'ITALIANA

This is our own version of gravlax, a Scandinavian dish in which salmon is traditionally cured with spruce or dill. We think the fennel and mint make an interesting change. Serve with Fennel-flavored Mustard Sauce (see page 268).

*1 whole salmon, about 3
    pounds*
2 tablespoons fennel seeds
3 tablespoons coarse salt
2 tablespoons sugar

*1 teaspoon freshly ground
    pepper*
*1 bunch wild fennel tops
    (optional)*
5 fresh mint sprigs, leaves only

Ask your fishmonger to fillet the salmon, leaving the skin on. Remove the pin bones from the fish, using a pliers or your fingers. Mix together in a small bowl the fennel seeds, salt, sugar, and white pepper. Place 1 fillet, skin-side down, in a glass or enamel baking dish. Rub the fennel seed mixture into the red flesh of the salmon. Lay the fennel tops and the mint leaves on top. Lay the second salmon fillet, skin-side down, on top of the first fillet. Cover the fish with wax paper, then cover the dish with plastic wrap. Set a plate on top of the fish and weight down with a heavy object of about 2 pounds. Let cure for 4 to 5 days in the refrigerator, turning the fish daily.

Before serving, lift the fish from the juices which will have collected in the pan. Remove the herbs from between the fillets and wipe the fillets dry. To serve, cut each fillet on the diagonal with a very thin, sharp knife into paper-thin slices. Serve on individual plates with a sauce for a first course, or serve on black bread as an appetizer. *Serves 30 to 40.*

P E S C E A L L I M O N E
f i s h i n l e m o n a n d c r e a m

Herring in sour cream has been a favorite for years. For those who are put off by its pungent taste, we developed this recipe to treat a milder fish in a similar manner. Radicchio leaves are beautiful in place of the lettuce leaves as a garnish.

1½ pounds sole, turbot, or cod
 fillets
Juice of 7 lemons
1½ cups heavy cream
½ cup sour cream
1–2 tablespoons snipped fresh
 chives

2 shallots or 1 small onion,
 peeled and thinly sliced
Coarse salt and freshly ground
 pepper to taste
Lettuce leaves, or radicchio
 leaves for garnish

For an entrée, leave the fillets whole. As a first course or hors d'oeuvre, cut the fish crosswise into 1-inch-wide slices. Place the fish in a glass or enamel bowl and pour the lemon juice over it. Cover with plastic wrap and marinate in the refrigerator at least 4 hours or overnight. Before serving, lightly whip the cream so that it has some body but is not stiff. Fold in the sour cream and 1 or 2 tablespoons of lemon juice from the fish. Gently fold in the chives, shallots, and a dash of salt and pepper. Set aside. Lift the fish out of the marinade. Arrange each whole fillet on a lettuce leaf and top with a spoonful or two of the cream mixture. For the appetizer or first course version, mix the fish slices with the cream mixture and arrange on lettuce leaves. *Serves 6 to 8 as a first course.*

SARDE SOTT'ACETO

marinated sardines

This is a strong, pungent dish that keeps for more than a week when refrigerated. It is worthwhile to double the amounts given here.

1 pound fresh sardines,
*   cleaned*
3 tablespoons plus ¼ cup olive
*   oil*
1 whole head garlic, cloves
*   separated and unpeeled*

3–4 bay leaves
1 teaspoon sweet paprika
1 cup wine vinegar

Sauté the sardines in the 3 tablespoons olive oil in a skillet. Set aside in a glass, enamel, or earthenware dish. For the marinade, brown the unpeeled garlic cloves in the ¼ cup olive oil in a medium skillet, adding the bay leaves. As soon as the garlic cloves are well browned, add the sweet paprika and stir for a minute or so. Add the vinegar and bring the mixture to a boil. Pour the boiling marinade over the sardines and let cool. Cover and let marinate in a cool place. *Serves 4 to 6 as an appetizer.*

SALMON SCALLOPS WITH BLACK PEPPERCORN VINAIGRETTE

We have discovered that this technique of "oven poaching" works well. It eliminates the need for court bouillion and elaborate utensils. In fact, we find the results to be superior in that flavor is retained and the fish is easier to handle.

The bite of the black peppercorns serves to offset some of the richness of the salmon. We use an Italian white wine vinegar that is actually pale peach in color, but any good-quality white wine vinegar will work well. This dish is simple to prepare and makes an elegant presentation.

1 teaspoon black peppercorns
¼ cup good-quality white wine vinegar
2 pounds salmon fillets, skinned

Coarse salt to taste
¼ cup dry white wine, or water
½ cup olive oil

Coarsely crush the peppercorns using a mortar and pestle. Combine the crushed peppercorns with the vinegar in a small bowl. Cover with plastic wrap and let marinate for 2 hours or longer. Pull out any bones that remain in the salmon fillets, using a pliers. Cut the fish on the bias with a sharp knife into six thin scallops. Lightly oil a shallow roasting pan. Lightly salt the fillets and place them in the pan and add the water or wine. Cover with parchment, wax paper, or oiled aluminum foil cut to fit just inside the pan. "Oven poach" in a preheated 450° oven for 7 to 10 minutes per inch of thickness. Remove from the oven and let the fish cool in the pan. Combine the olive oil, the vinegar and crushed peppercorn mixture, and salt. To serve, spoon a little of the vinaigrette with some of the crushed peppercorns over the salmon. *Serves 4 to 6.*

SALMON SCALLOPS WITH CAVIAR

This salmon dish lends itself to an elegant presentation.

2 pounds salmon fillets, skinned
Coarse salt to taste
¼ cup dry white wine, or water
½ cup Lemon Mayonnaise (see page 265)

4–8 ounces golden caviar (whitefish roe)
Tomato Halves with Parsley Sauce (see page 172)
1 recipe Insalata Russa (see page 66)
1 cup cornichons

Slice the salmon and oven poach with the white wine as described in Salmon Scallops with Black Peppercorn Vinaigrette (see page 182). Serve each salmon scallop with a dollop of Lemon Mayonnaise topped with a spoonful of caviar. Accompany with Tomato Halves with Parsley Sauce, Insalata Russa, and cornichons. *Serves 6.*

TROUT MARINATED WITH SAGE

Let the fish marinate for many hours so the pungent sage flavor permeates the delicate flesh of the trout. Cooking *al cartoccio* (sealed in paper or foil) helps the fish retain its moisture after it cools.

4 whole river trout, 1½–2 pounds each, cleaned and scaled, head on or off
1 tablespoon coarse salt
2 teaspoons freshly ground pepper

2 bunches fresh sage leaves, or 2 tablespoons dried sage leaves, crumbled
Juice of 2 lemons
½ cup olive oil

Wash trout and pat dry with paper towels. Cut three diagonal slashes deep into the flesh on each side of fish. Rub salt and pepper into each fish, seasoning both the slashes and the cavity. Place the fish in an enamel or glass dish large enough to hold them in 1 layer. Remove the stems from the sage and coarsely chop enough leaves to measure ¼ cup. Mix in a small bowl the lemon juice, olive oil, and sage. Pour the marinade over the fish so that it coats the fish completely and penetrates the gashes on both sides of the fish. Cover with plastic wrap and refrigerate for 3 to 12 hours, turning occasionally.

When ready to cook, place each fish in the center of a piece of oiled aluminum foil. Decorate each fish with fresh whole sage leaves over each gash on the presentation side. Distribute any extra marinade among the fish packets. Wrap the foil to make packets, pleating the edges to seal securely. Place the fish packets on a baking sheet and bake in a preheated 400° oven for 10 minutes per inch of thickness.

Remove from oven and carefully open the foil packets. Let cool. Strain the juices from the packets. Present fish whole with 1 tablespoon reserved juices over each. Serve at room temperature. *Serves 4.*

S G O M B R O   A L L ' A G R O
marinated mackerel

The rich, oily quality of mackerel is perfectly suited to this preparation using vinegar and wine. A satisfying and tangy dish.

2 pounds mackerel fillets, or 2 cans (1 pound each) mackerel

¼ cup lemon juice

Coarse salt and freshly ground pepper to taste

Dash cayenne pepper, or chili powder

1 onion, peeled and thinly sliced

2 carrots, peeled and cut into ¼-inch rounds

1 large green bell pepper, cored, seeded, and thinly sliced

6 garlic cloves, peeled and thinly sliced

3 tablespoons olive oil

1 cup white wine

½ cup white wine vinegar

½ cup water

½ teaspoon whole black peppercorns

½ teaspoon whole coriander seeds

Place each mackerel fillet on a sheet of oiled aluminum foil. Fold the foil into a packet, pleating the edges to seal. Place on a baking sheet and bake in a preheated 350° oven for 10 minutes or until the fillets are just cooked through. Remove from the oven, open the packets, and let cool. Remove any bones. Place the fillets in a glass or enamel baking or serving dish. Sprinkle with the lemon juice, salt, pepper, and cayenne.

Sauté the onion, carrot, green pepper, and garlic in the olive oil in a medium skillet for 5 minutes. Add the white wine, vinegar, water, salt, peppercorns, and coriander. Simmer until the vegetables are just tender. Pour over the mackerel. Let cool. Cover with plastic wrap and refrigerate for at least 24 hours. Serve at room temperature. *Serves 4 to 6.*

GRILLED SWORDFISH WITH SALSA CRUDA

Swordfish can dry out very easily. To avoid this we use thin steaks and quick grilling. Grilling adds wonderful flavor to the swordfish, but it can also be done successfully in a broiler. Salsa Cruda adds fresh flavor and a bright splash of color.

2 pounds swordfish, cut into large ½-inch-thick steaks
Olive oil

Coarse salt and freshly ground pepper to taste
1 recipe Salsa Cruda (see page 271)

Brush the steaks with olive oil. Grill very close to the source of heat, about 4 to 5 minutes total cooking time, turning once. Place the fish on a serving dish and season with salt and pepper. Spoon some of the Salsa Cruda over the fish and let cool. Do not refrigerate. Serve with extra sauce on the side. *Serves 4.*

WHOLE FISH FLAVORED WITH HERB PASTE

Use coarse salt, which helps the herbs and garlic break down to a paste and release their flavor and aroma. Serve simply with lemon wedges or with Lemon Mayonnaise (see page 265). Use a generous amount of coarse salt to make the paste, at least 2 teaspoons.

1 whole fish, 3–3½ pounds, such as red snapper, cleaned with head and tail left on, washed and patted dry
3 garlic cloves, peeled
2 tablespoons chopped fresh mint leaves

1 teaspoon dried oregano leaves, crumbled
Coarse salt and freshly ground pepper to taste
1 cup dry white wine
Fresh sprigs of mint and oregano for garnish (optional)

Cut three diagonal slices into the flesh on each side of fish. Make a paste with the garlic, mint, oregano, salt, and pepper by chopping the ingredients together until very fine, and repeatedly pressing down with the flat side of a chef's knife; or use a mortar and pestle. Rub the interior and exterior of the fish with the herb paste, being careful to work the seasonings into the slashes. Place the fish in an enamel or glass baking dish and pour the wine over. Cover tightly with aluminum foil. Cook the fish in a preheated 450° oven for 10 minutes per inch of thickness (measuring the fish depth at its thickest point) until the flesh is firm and opaque. Let cool. Skin before serving. To serve, cut into chunks along top fillet. Remove the backbone and repeat with the bottom fillet. If desired, garnish the fish with fresh sprigs of mint and oregano. *Serves 6.*

CONDIGLIONE
fresh tuna salad

Condiglione is a salad from the Italian Riviera. Its fresh flavors evoke memories of terraced vegetable gardens overlooking the sea and the scent of basil in the air. In our version of this salad, we have expanded the role of the tuna, using fresh instead of canned. The preliminary marination helps ensure that the fish remains meltingly tender.

1 cup fruity olive oil

3 tablespoons lemon juice

¼ medium red onion, peeled and sliced

6 garlic cloves, peeled and lightly crushed

3 fresh parsley sprigs

3 whole cloves

1 pound fresh tuna, cut in 1-inch-thick pieces

Coarse salt and freshly ground pepper to taste

2 bell peppers, red or yellow, smooth and evenly formed

1 bunch green onions, wilted layers removed and root ends trimmed

1 medium hot-house cucumber, peeled, halved, seeded, and cut crosswise into ⅛-inch-thick slices

6 medium tomatoes, peeled, cored, and cut into wedges

3 canned flat anchovy fillets, chopped into small pieces

1 bunch fresh basil, about 20 leaves

4 hard-cooked eggs

½ cup oil-cured black olives

Make a marinade by combining 3 tablespoons of the olive oil, the lemon juice, sliced red onion, 3 of the garlic cloves, parsley, and cloves in a glass or enamel baking dish. Moisten both sides of the tuna in the marinade and lightly salt and pepper. Cover with plastic wrap and refrigerate for 2 or 3 hours, turning the fish over once at a halfway point. Bring to room temperature before cooking. Cook the tuna, covered, in 3 tablespoons of the olive oil in a large skillet over very low heat, about 3 minutes on each side until just done. It should be slightly pink at the center. Let cool to room temperature. Remove the skin and break the tuna into large chunks using a fork. Very gently toss with ¼ cup of the olive oil in a large bowl.

Peel the bell peppers with a very sharp vegetable peeler or a paring knife. It may be easier to cut the pepper into wedges first and then peel. (Peeling the peppers is a refinement that is not absolutely necessary, but it is an improvement if you do not care for the tough skin.) Remove the seeds and membranes. Cut in ¼-inch-wide julienne. Cut off the dark green tops from the green onions, leaving a little of the tender green part. Slice into thin rounds. In a large bowl, combine the tuna, bell pepper, green onion, cucumber, tomato, anchovy, and remaining garlic cloves. Tear the basil leaves into pieces and sprinkle over the salad. Drizzle with remaining 6 tablespoons olive oil. Add salt and pepper. Toss very gently, cover with plastic wrap, and let marinate for 1 hour. Before serving the salad, peel eggs and cut lengthwise into quarters. Taste the salad and adjust the seasonings. Remove the garlic cloves. Mound the salad on a platter. Surround with the quartered hard-cooked eggs and the olives. *Serves 4.*

GRILLED TUNA WITH TOMATO GARNISH

We think the sharp taste of arugola and the mellow piquancy of balsamic vinegar are an inspired foil to the rich taste of fresh tuna.

3 pounds fresh tuna, cut into slices no thicker than ½ inch
Olive oil
6 small tomatoes, stems removed, diced fine
3 tablespoons large Spanish capers

2 tablespoons fruity olive oil
Balsamic vinegar to taste
2 bunches arugola, washed and stems removed
Freshly ground pepper to taste

Brush the tuna slices lightly with olive oil. Grill on a hot, oiled outdoor grill or in a preheated hot broiler for about 5 minutes, turning once. Do not overcook; the fish will continue to cook for 1 or 2 minutes even after you remove it from the grill. Remove the fish to a platter to cool. To make the garnish, mix the tomatoes, capers, olive oil, and vinegar in a small bowl. Before serving, line individual plates with a bed of arugola leaves. Place the grilled tuna on the arugola and garnish with 2 tablespoons or so of the tomato mixture. Grind black pepper over the top of each dish. *Serves 6.*

INSALATA DI MARE
seafood salad

The flavors and colors come together to create an exquisite experience. Bright strips of red bell pepper against shiny black mussel shells; coral-colored shrimp and tender green basil; pure white circles of squid; pink-tinged morsels of scallops; and thin bands of lemon. Fresh essence of the sea. Although best if made a few hours before serving and never seeing the inside of a refrigerator, it can be made a day or two in advance with great success.

1 pound medium shrimp
1 pound squid
½ pound bay or sea scallops
2 pounds mussels, the smaller the better
4 large garlic cloves, peeled and cut in half
1 roasted peeled red bell pepper, cut into strips (see page 93)

¼ cup Niçoise olives or black oil-cured olives
¾ cup fruity olive oil
½ cup lemon juice
10 fresh basil leaves
Coarse salt and freshly ground pepper to taste
½ lemon, thinly sliced

Leave the shells on the shrimp. Devein by cutting along the outside curve of the shell. Rinse under cold running water. Bring a large pot of salted water to a boil. Add the shrimp and cook just until opaque, 2 to 4 minutes. Drain. Let cool. Discard the shells.

To clean the squid, carefully pull the head and tentacles from the body sac. Cut the tentacles above the eyes. Pop out the little ball or beak in the center of the tentacles. Discard it and the innards. Pull out the quill-shaped bone in the body sac and discard. Peel off the skin. Thoroughly rinse the interior of the body and the tentacles. Drain. Cook in the same way as the shrimp. After 20 minutes, test for tenderness. Drain. Cut crosswise into rings. Cut the tentacles in half if large.

Leave bay scallops whole; cut sea scallops into quarters. Repeat cooking procedure as for the shrimp and squid. Check after 2 or 3 minutes. They should be barely opaque at the center. Drain and let cool.

Scrub the mussels well under cold running water. Remove all traces of grit and slime. The mussels in the shell will be used in the salad. Remove the beard by tugging hard at it until it breaks free from the shell. Discard any shells that are open or cracked. Place in a wide-bottomed pan. Add a few tablespoons of water. Cover and cook over high heat, shaking the pan while cooking to redistribute the mussels. When the mussels open, remove from the pan and let cool.

To assemble the salad, combine the seafood with the garlic, red bell pepper strips, Niçoise olives, olive oil, and lemon juice in a large bowl. Tear the basil leaves into pieces and add to the salad. Toss gently, adding salt and pepper. Cover tightly with plastic wrap and marinate for 2 hours. If refrigerated, bring to room temperature before serving. Remove the garlic. Adjust seasonings, adding more olive oil, lemon juice, salt, and pepper, if needed. Garnish with lemon slices. *Serves 4 to 6.*

CRAB IN LEMON DRESSING

Crab has a sweet, light flavor. Our suggested garnishes add little touches of jewel-like color and bright flavor accents, but even without them the crab is just as delightful.

2 large crabs, cooked, cleaned, and cracked
Fruity olive oil
Lemon juice
Coarse salt and freshly ground pepper to taste
Lemon wedges
Fresh flat-leaf parsley sprigs

Red and yellow tomatoes, peeled, seeded, and cut into small dice (optional)
Capers
Basil leaves
Lemon Mayonnaise (see page 265)

Set aside the crab legs. Remove the meat from the crab body. Gently toss the crab meat with a little olive oil and lemon juice in a medium bowl. Season with salt and pepper. Mound a little of the dressed crab in the center of each of 4 plates. Surround each mound of crab with crab legs. Garnish with lemon wedges and flat-leaf parsley. If desired, omit the parsley and toss crab meat with diced red and yellow tomatoes. Sprinkle with capers and basil torn into little pieces. Serve with a little dollop of Lemon Mayonnaise on each plate. Supply nutcrackers, if necessary. *Serves 4 as a light first course.*

SHRIMP MARINATED IN WILD FENNEL

Wild fennel grows on the hillsides in Southern California. Its feathery leaves and tender stalks add a licorice flavor to foods. Marinate the salad at least overnight and up to three days. Flavors intensify with longer marination. Serve with a little of the flavored olive oil drizzled over the shrimp.

2 pounds medium shrimp, lightly cooked, peeled, and deveined (see page 191)

1 cup coarsely chopped wild fennel tops and stalks, or 1 cup coarsely chopped fennel bulb

2 lemons, thinly sliced

½ teaspoon crushed dried red chile pepper

1 tablespoon fennel seeds

6 garlic cloves, peeled and sliced

Coarse salt and freshly ground pepper to taste

Fruity olive oil

8 bay leaves

Alternate layers of shrimp, fennel, and lemon slices in a glass or enamel bowl. Season each layer of shrimp with the dried red chile pepper, fennel seeds, garlic, salt, and pepper. Add olive oil to cover. Arrange the bay leaves over the top and cover with plastic wrap. Marinate overnight in the refrigerator. Allow to come to room temperature before serving. *Serves 4 to 6.*

SHRIMP IN SPICY LIME MARINADE

This can be part of a fun participation meal as each guest shells his own shrimp. Provide a container for shells and pass out large napkins. Provide lemon-scented water in fingerbowls after the meal for those who wish to tidy up.

1½–2 pounds shrimp, medium to large
Coarse salt to taste
Juice of 3 lemons
Juice of 4 limes
6 whole garlic cloves, peeled and cut in half

¼ teaspoon dried red pepper flakes, or 3–4 small dried red chiles, broken in half
¼ cup olive oil
Lemon and lime wedges
Freshly ground pepper

Devein the shrimp, leaving the shells on (see page 191). The shells will be loose but should remain on. Dry the shrimp with paper towels, sprinkle with salt, and place in a glass, enamel, or stainless steel bowl. Mix together the lemon and lime juices, garlic, and red pepper in a small bowl. Pour the marinade over the shrimp, cover with plastic wrap, refrigerate, and allow to marinate at least 4 hours. This can be done a day ahead. When ready to cook, lift the shrimp from the marinade, brush with olive oil, and either grill on a hot barbecue or place in a preheated broiler about 4 inches from the source of heat, about 7 minutes, turning once. While the shrimp cooks, mix the remaining marinade with olive oil. Use as a dipping sauce. Serve the shrimp with lemon and lime wedges and freshly ground pepper. Guests shell their own shrimp. *Serves 4.*

MUSSELS WITH SPICY TOMATO AND BASIL SAUCE

Try to find small, tender mussels. The sauce is cooked very quickly to maintain the fresh tomato flavor, and only a small amount of sauce is used to accent the mussels. The contrast of jet black shells and bright red tomato sauce is visually very striking.

4 pounds mussels
Dry white wine, or water
3 tablespoons olive oil
*1 large garlic clove, peeled
    and minced*
*½ teaspoon crushed dried red
    chile peppers*
*4 tomatoes, peeled, seeded,
    chopped, and drained, or
    1 cup canned imported
    Italian tomatoes, seeded,
    chopped fine, and drained*

*1 tablespoon minced fresh
    basil leaves, or 1 teaspoon
    dried basil leaves,
    crumbled*
1 tablespoon lemon juice
*1 tablespoon grated lemon
    rind*
Coarse salt to taste

Scrub the mussels well under cold running water, making sure shells are completely free of sand and grit. Remove the beards that protrude from the shells, by tugging hard until they come out. Discard any mussels that are broken or not firmly clamped shut. Place the mussels in a large, wide-bottomed pot and add dry white wine or water to a depth of ½ inch in the bottom of the pot. Cover and cook over high heat, shaking the pan while cooking to redistribute the mussels, until the mussels open. It will only take a few minutes. Remove the pot from the heat as soon as the mussels open or they will toughen. With a slotted spoon, lift the mussels from the pot into a bowl and reserve the juices. Working over the bowl containing the cooked mussels, remove the half shell that does not contain the mussel, catching the juices in the bowl. Put mussels in their half shell on a platter and cover with plastic wrap while you make the sauce. Add the juices from the bowl to the juices in the pot. Boil until the liquid is reduced by half. Strain through several layers of dampened cheesecloth.

Combine the olive oil, garlic, and dried chile pepper in a medium skillet. Sauté over low heat for 2 or 3 minutes, making sure the garlic does not brown. When very fragrant, add the chopped tomatoes, increase the heat to medium, and cook until the mixture thickens and the liquid from the tomatoes has evaporated, about 4 minutes. Turn off the heat. Add the basil, lemon juice, lemon rind, and enough of the reduced mussel liquid to flavor the sauce without it becoming too salty. Taste for salt. Spoon a small amount of the sauce into each mussel. *Serves 4.*

MUSSELS IN WHITE WINE AND GARLIC

Serve with hot crostini (see page 9) drizzled with olive oil and rubbed with garlic. When cooking, remove the mussels just as they open to preserve the briny, fresh flavor and tenderness.

4 pounds mussels
Dry white wine or water
3 tablespoons olive oil
4 garlic cloves, peeled and
    minced
1 tablespoon minced fresh flat-
    leaf parsley

Coarse salt and freshly ground
    pepper to taste
Juice of 1 or 2 lemons
Lemon wedges

Scrub the mussels well under cold running water. Remove the beard by tugging hard at it until it breaks from the shell. Discard any mussels that are open or cracked. Place the mussels in a large wide-bottomed pot and add wine or water to a depth of ½ inch in the bottom of the pot. Cover and cook over high heat. Shake the pan from time to time to redistribute the mussels. As they open, remove them to a bowl to keep them from toughening. Remove the top shell from each mussel over the bowl containing the cooked mussels. Combine the mussel liquid in the pan with the liquid in the bowl. Strain through several layers of dampened cheesecloth.

Heat the olive oil, garlic, and parsley in a skillet over low heat. When the garlic releases its fragrance, 2 to 3 minutes, add the strained mussel liquid. Season with salt and pepper, and simmer for several minutes to concentrate the flavors. Cool. Arrange the mussels on a platter. Spoon a little of the cooled liquid into each shell. Sprinkle with lemon juice. Cover tightly with plastic wrap until needed. Serve with lemon wedges on the side. *Serves 4.*

STUFFED SQUID

⅓ cup long-grain white rice
8 large squid
1 cup olive oil
2 garlic cloves, peeled and
    minced
3 tablespoons minced fresh
    parsley
1 carrot, peeled and cut into
    small dice

1 celery stalk, peeled and
    minced
1 tomato, peeled, seeded, and
    coarsely chopped
Coarse salt and freshly ground
    pepper to taste
Dry white wine or water, as
    needed
Lemon wedges

Cook the rice in an abundant amount of boiling salted water in a saucepan until al dente, about 10 minutes. Drain. If you have not bought cleaned squid, clean them according to directions on page 191. Chop the tentacles. Reserve the bodies. Let drain. Heat 3 tablespoons of the olive oil with the garlic and parsley in a skillet over low heat. Add the carrot and celery and cook until tender, about 15 minutes. Add the tomato, chopped tentacles, salt, and pepper and cook for 2 or 3 minutes or until the tentacles are opaque. Add the rice and stir to mix. Adjust the seasonings. Turn off the heat. Stuff the squid bodies about half full with the rice mixture. Fasten the open end with toothpicks. Lightly oil a baking dish just large enough to contain the squid in one layer. Pour the remaining oil over the squid and season lightly with salt and pepper. Cook in a preheated 350° oven for 45 minutes or until the squid is tender when pierced with the tip of a knife. Baste squid as it cooks, adding a little white wine or water, if necessary. Cool the squid in the juices in the baking dish. Serve the squid whole, or cut into ½-inch rings, with a little of the pan juice and the lemon wedges. *Serves 4.*

INSALATA DI CALAMARI

squid salad in mint and basil vinaigrette

A refreshing, fragrant salad with tender squid, diced potatoes, and fresh tomato in a vinaigrette. Fresh basil and mint give this seafood salad a marvelous summery feeling. Buy the smallest squid available and cook it until it loses all traces of rubberiness. Squid is exceedingly tender when properly cooked. To keep the flesh pure white, cook the body of the squid separately from the tentacles, since the skin of the tentacles releases color into the cooking water which will turn the flesh a pale pink. This salad can be made several hours in advance.

2½ pounds squid
Juice of ½ lemon
½ cup fruity olive oil
4 tablespoons white wine vinegar
3 garlic cloves, peeled and lightly crushed
Coarse salt and freshly ground pepper to taste

3 large boiling potatoes
2 large tomatoes
1 tablespoon minced fresh basil leaves
2 teaspoons minced fresh mint leaves

Clean the squid as directed on page 191. Cook the body and tentacles in boiling salted water in 2 separate saucepans with lemon juice for 20 minutes or until tender. Drain well. Cut the body into rings. Leave the tentacles whole or, if large, cut in half. Combine the squid in a large bowl with the olive oil, vinegar, garlic, salt, and pepper. Cover and marinate overnight in the refrigerator. The next day cook the potatoes in boiling salted water to cover in a saucepan until tender but firm. Drain. When cool enough to handle, peel. When cold, cut into 1-inch dice. Peel and seed the tomatoes, then cut them into strips. Put the potatoes and tomatoes on a platter. Add the squid and marinade. Sprinkle with the herbs. Toss gently, seasoning with salt and pepper. Adjust the dressing, adding more oil and vinegar if necessary. *Serves 4 to 6.*

SIMPLE BOILED LOBSTER

Serve lobster with lemon or lime wedges, Lemon Mayonnaise (see page 265), or Salsa Cruda (see page 271).

4 live lobsters, each 1–1½
     pounds
Coarse salt

Bring a very large pot of water to a boil. Add salt. Let the water return to a brisk boil. Plunge the lobsters head first into the water. Cook only as many as fit easily in the pot. Cook for 6 to 8 minutes for 1-pound lobster, and 8 to 10 minutes for 1½-pound lobster. Remove from the boiling water. Let drain and cool. Split the lobsters in half, cutting from the head to the tail on the underside. Remove and discard the intestinal vein close to the back. Crack claws and let drain. Arrange on a platter and serve with any of the above mentioned garnishes or sauces. *Serves 4.*

LOBSTER AND ROASTED RED PEPPER SALAD

The pure white of the lobster set against the lustrous red of the bell peppers is especially beautiful. Both the lobster and the red bell peppers have a fresh, sweet flavor; a sophisticated treat.

1 large cooked meaty lobster tail, split
2 red bell peppers
¼ cup fruity olive oil
Juice of 1 lemon

3 garlic cloves, peeled and lightly crushed
Coarse salt and freshly ground pepper to taste
1 teaspoon capers

Remove the lobster meat from the shell. Cut into generous chunks. Roast the red peppers over a stovetop burner or under a preheated broiler, using tongs to turn the peppers until they are completely blackened. Place them immediately into a plastic bag. Close the bag and let them sweat for 10 minutes. Peel the peppers carefully under cold running water. Place on paper towels to dry. Cut the peppers in half and remove the seeds and membranes. Cut lengthwise into ½-inch-wide strips. Combine the lobster, red pepper, olive oil, lemon juice, and garlic cloves in a medium bowl. Add the salt and pepper. Cover with plastic wrap and let marinate in the refrigerator for several hours. Toss very gently once or twice. Before serving, allow to come to room temperature. Adjust the seasonings, adding more lemon juice if necessary. Remove the garlic cloves. Arrange on a platter and sprinkle with capers. *Serves 2.*

Oysters

Few foods are as simultaneously simple, festive, and sensuous as the oyster. We find it liberating to occasionally go without cooking and to instead entertain by setting up an oyster bar.

Oysters can be bought one or two days ahead. Simply store them in the refrigerator, convex shell down so they can bathe in their own juices, covered with a damp cloth. Never store oysters in water. Oysters eaten on the half shell are eaten live so it is important to carefully choose the bivalves. Discard any that are light or too heavy as these are most likely dead or filled with mud. Most oysters keep their shells tightly closed when out of water. If the shells are slightly opened, touch them. A live oyster will quickly close his shell.

Shuck the oysters using an oyster knife. Hold the oyster, convex shell down, in a heavy towel to protect your hand. Force the tip of the oyster knife into the hinge, then twist the knife to pry open the shells. Once the shell pops open, slide the knife alongside the upper shell to sever the oyster from the shell. Discard the top shell and slip the knife under the oyster to loosen it from the lower shell.

For an informal gathering of close friends, set up the oyster bar in your kitchen, filling the sink with ice. For a more elegant presentation, lay the oysters on large platters filled with crushed ice. Precede the oysters with an appetizer of fresh caviar. We prefer our oysters with a squeeze of lemon and some freshly ground pepper. Other accompaniments are: lime wedges, minced fresh chile peppers, Tabasco sauce, minced fresh cilantro, basil, chives, or any herb vinegar. Serve oysters with thin slices of buttered black or rye bread and champagne or white wine.

SPICY OYSTER SALAD

There are lots of contrasts of flavor and texture in this salad: the smooth, briny flavor of the oysters on a bed of rough, slightly bitter endive, dressed with the spicy citrus flavor of lime juice and chiles.

30 oysters, 5 per person, scrubbed

3 small tender carrots, peeled, ends trimmed, and cut crosswise into thin rounds

1 head curly endive lettuce

DRESSING:

½ cup light olive oil
Juice of 1 large lemon
Juice of 2 large limes
2 tablespoons minced fresh parsley leaves
1–2 small red chiles, stemmed, seeded, and minced

Coarse salt and freshly ground pepper to taste
1 tablespoon clam juice (optional)
⅛ pound or 1 package spicy radish or daikon sprouts

Grill the scrubbed oysters by placing them, deep shell side down, on a sheet of aluminum foil which has been placed directly on hot coals, until the shells pop open, 2 to 4 minutes. Be careful not to overcook. Remove the oysters from the shells over a bowl, reserving the liquor. Blanch the carrot rounds briefly in boiling salted water in a small saucepan for 30 seconds. Drain in a colander and refresh under cold running water. Place on paper towels to dry. Wash the endive lettuce, discarding the tough outer leaves. Cut out and discard core. Tear the lettuce leaves into bite-size pieces. Dry on paper towels.

To prepare the dressing, whisk together the olive oil, lemon and lime juices, parsley, chiles, salt, and pepper. Strain any reserved oyster liquor through a triple layer of dampened cheesecloth, and add to the dressing. If the oysters have not yielded sufficient liquor, add the optional clam juice. To serve, toss the endive in a bowl with just enough dressing to moisten the leaves. Place small amounts of dressed endive on individual salad plates. Sprinkle with a few carrot rounds. Dip each oyster in the remaining dressing, and arrange 5 to a plate on top of the lettuce. Garnish with the sprouts. *Serves 6 as a salad course.*

meat and poultry

CARPACCIO WITH HERBS AND LEMON JUICE

Many people are at first put off by the idea of eating uncooked beef. However, the first experience with a simple dish like Carpaccio is enough to convert anyone. Eating a small portion of uncooked meat is healthful, light on the palate and the stomach while being extremely satisfying. It is what we term a "clean" food. It is most frequently served in Italy covered with thin slices of fresh Parmesan and moistened with a good olive oil, but the variations are endless. What follows are two of what we consider to be the freshest and most satisfying versions. Other suggestions are to serve Carpaccio with a Black Peppercorn Vinaigrette (see page 182) or with a Basil

Mayonnaise (see page 266). During summer months when hot weather demands light eating, we often serve Carpaccio as an entrée with a light first course and a salad course to follow, but it is most often served as a first course.

*1½ pounds fillet of beef,
    cleaned of all fat and
    membrane*
*Coarse salt and freshly ground
    pepper to taste*
*5 sprigs fresh flat-leaf parsley,
    leaves minced*

*5 sprigs fresh basil leaves,
    minced*
Fruity olive oil
2 lemons

Place the meat in the freezer for 15 minutes. It should be firm enough to slice thinly. Use a sharp knife to cut through the partially frozen meat. If you prefer, ask your butcher to slice the meat for you. Carpaccio is sometimes served paper thin. We prefer it to be closer to ⅛ inch thick. In other words, it should be only thick enough to hold its shape when lifted with the fork. Keep in mind that if you plan to keep the sliced beef awhile before serving, it should be tightly wrapped in plastic wrap to prevent the meat from darkening. When ready to serve, cover each individual plate with overlapping slices of the uncooked, thinly sliced beef. Sprinkle salt, pepper, and herbs to taste on the beef. Lightly drizzle olive oil and lemon juice on top. *Serves 6 to 8 as a first course.*

CARPACCIO WITH ARUGOLA AND PARMESAN

*1 ½ pounds fillet of beef,
   cleaned of all fat and
   membrane*
2 bunches arugola

*½ pound Parmesan in one
   piece*
Freshly ground pepper to taste
Fruity olive oil

Follow the directions in preceding recipe for preparing the beef. Carefully clean the arugola of sand and discard any yellowed leaves. Cut off and discard stems and tear each leaf in half crosswise. Using a truffle slicer, a mandoline, or a sharp knife, cut the Parmesan into very thin slices. Arrange the beef on individual plates, overlapping the slices slightly. Grind fresh black pepper over the meat. Cover the meat with the arugola leaves and slices of Parmesan, except for a ring of pink around the edge of the plate. Drizzle with olive oil. *Serves 6 to 8 as a first course.*

FLORENTINE GRILLED STEAK

"Steak, perfectly broiled, seasoned, cooled and sliced thin is even more succulent than steak rushed from the grill," observes James Beard. This must be grilled over natural charcoal to get close to the flavor of a true Florentine grill.

**2 very large T-bone or
    Porterhouse steaks, about
    2 inches thick
Coarse salt and freshly ground
    pepper to taste**

**Lemon wedges
Cruet of fruity olive oil**

Bring the meat to room temperature. Prepare a very hot charcoal grill using natural wood charcoal. Place the unseasoned meat on a very hot grill close to the source of heat. Cook until very crusty on the outside and quite rare inside, 15 minutes in total, turning once and salting the cooked side. Grind fresh pepper over the meat and let cool a little. Slice very thin. Serve with lemon wedges and a small cruet of olive oil. *Serves 4.*

GRILLED FLANK STEAK

Flank steak should be grilled very rare, red on the inside and charred on the outside, to be really tender and flavorful. If desired, add a little orange peel to the marinade. Serve grilled and sliced flank steak with Black Peppercorn Vinaigrette (see page 182) or with Aïoli (see page 267). Or accompany with the marinade served as a dipping sauce.

1 flank steak, about 2 pounds
1 cup dry red wine
¼ cup soy sauce
4 garlic cloves, peeled and
  lightly crushed

Coarse salt and freshly ground
  pepper to taste

Lightly pound the flank steak with a rolling pin to tenderize the meat. Combine the remaining ingredients for the marinade in a shallow dish just large enough to hold the flank steak. Put the meat in marinade and cover. Marinate, refrigerated, from 2 hours to overnight. Turn the meat occasionally in the marinade. Remove the meat from the marinade. Pat dry. Grill over very hot coals or under a very hot broiler for about 4 minutes on each side, basting with the marinade as it cooks and seasoning with salt and pepper. Let cool a little. Slice thinly on an extreme diagonal or the meat will be less tender. Serve at room temperature without refrigerating. To serve the marinade as a dipping sauce, bring the marinade to a boil in a saucepan and reduce by one-quarter. Let cool before serving. *Serves 4.*

INSALATA BISTECCA
steak salad

This is a lighter approach to a beef main course. A versatile dish, it can be the basis for a simple light lunch or served within the context of a full-course meal. We like the way the charred flavor of the steak marries with the mustardy vinaigrette.

2 pounds sirloin steak
1 pound white mushrooms
1 bunch green onions,
    trimmed

2 firm ripe tomatoes, peeled
    and seeded
2 tablespoons minced fresh
    parsley

DRESSING:

½ cup olive oil
3 tablespoons red wine vinegar
1 tablespoon Dijon or other
    strong mustard
1 garlic clove, peeled and put
    through press

1 small shallot, peeled and
    minced (optional)
Coarse salt and freshly ground
    pepper to taste
Lettuce leaves

Place the steak in a preheated hot broiler about 4 inches from the flame. Cook approximately 3 minutes on each side, depending on the thickness of steak. Steak should be on the rare side. Remove to a plate to cool. If possible, do not refrigerate before using as the steak will dry out somewhat. While the steak is cooling, wipe the mushrooms clean with a damp cloth and trim the stem ends. If the stems are particularly woody, discard them. Slice the mushrooms thinly with a sharp knife. Cut the green onions, discarding the green tops, into paper-thin rings. Cut the tomatoes into ½-inch dice. When the steak has cooled to room temperature, cut it against the grain into ¼-inch-thick slices. If the slices are particularly long, cut them in half crosswise. Combine the sliced steak with the mushrooms, green onions, tomatoes, and parsley in a large bowl. Set aside.

To prepare the dressing, combine the olive oil, vinegar, mustard, garlic, shallot if desired, salt, and pepper in a small bowl. Beat with a whisk and pour over the steak salad mixture. Toss gently and serve on lettuce leaves. *Serves 4 to 6 as a luncheon entrée.*

MARINATED COOKED BEEF

This dish is also a delicious and elegant way to use leftover rare roast beef. In fact, when pressed for time, you can buy thinly sliced *rare* roast beef from a good delicatessen and prepare it in the same manner.

2 pounds tenderloin of beef
Coarse salt and freshly ground
pepper to taste
¼ cup olive oil
1 bunch fresh sage leaves,
coarsely chopped

1 bunch fresh thyme, woody
lower stems removed
Fresh thyme sprigs

Have your butcher trim the meat of all visible fat and sinews. Generously rub salt and pepper all over the roast. Rub 1 tablespoon of oil over the meat and place in a shallow roasting pan. Roast the tenderloin in a preheated 450° oven for 10 to 15 minutes or until a meat thermometer registers 140°. This roast is at its best when very rare. Let the meat cool in its juices. Refrigerate before slicing to facilitate slicing very thin. When the roast is cold enough to slice easily, cut into thin slices. Place a layer of slices in an enamel or glass dish. Scatter some of the herbs, salt, and pepper over the meat and sprinkle with enough oil to just moisten the meat. Continue layering the meat with herbs, salt, pepper, and oil. Cover with plastic wrap and refrigerate for at least 3 hours and as much as 12 hours. When ready to serve, arrange the circles of beef in an overlapping pattern on a serving platter. Garnish with fresh thyme sprigs. *Serves 4 to 8.*

BRISKET OF BEEF WITH PIQUANT PARSLEY SAUCE AND GIARDINIERA

This is a wonderful main course, tangy and vivid. Arrange the slices of beef on a platter. Spoon the bright green sauce over the beef. Surround with the giardiniera (pickled red bell pepper, carrot, cauliflower, and cucumber) cut into small julienne. Make sure you buy the mild giardiniera as opposed to the hot variety.

1 beef brisket, about 4 pounds
4 tablespoons olive oil
1 onion, peeled and coarsely chopped
2 carrots, peeled, trimmed, and sliced
2 celery stalks, peeled and sliced
1 garlic clove, peeled and minced
Freshly ground pepper to taste
Boiling water, or broth

FOR PARSLEY SAUCE:

1 garlic clove, peeled and minced
4 canned flat anchovies, minced
¼ cup minced fresh parsley leaves, about half a bunch
2 tablespoons capers, drained, rinsed, and minced
5 large fresh basil leaves, minced
4 tablespoons lemon juice
6 tablespoons fruity olive oil
1 jar (16 ounces) mild giardiniera for garnish

Sear the brisket in the oil in a roasting pan or Dutch oven with lid, browning all sides. When the meat is nicely browned, remove it to a platter. Turn the heat to medium and add the vegetables, garlic, and a few grinds of pepper. Stir the vegetables until they begin to color. Pour off any excess fat from the pan. Return the brisket to the pan, laying it on top of the vegetables. Add boiling water or broth to a depth of ½ inch. Cover the pan tightly and place either in a preheated 325° oven or cook on top of the stove over medium heat for about 2½ hours, or until a fork easily penetrates the meat. Check the meat occasionally to see that the liquid has not completely evaporated, adding more boiling water or broth as necessary. Allow the brisket to cool overnight in its own juices. Before serving, remove all the fat and cut the meat into slices about ¼ inch thick.

To make the Parsley Sauce, combine the garlic, anchovies, parsley, capers, basil, lemon juice, and olive oil in a small bowl. To serve, arrange the meat on a platter. Spoon the Parsley Sauce over the meat. Cut the giardiniera into matchstick julienne and place around the beef. *Serves 4 to 6.*

PICKLED BEEF

Slow roasting and a piquant marination lend tenderness to a normally tough cut of meat. An alternative to the roasting of chuck is to boil an eye of round or brisket. Cool, slice, and marinate the meat in the manner described below. The sweet, pickled flavor is complemented by serving it with big green olives, boiled potatoes, and artichokes with Anchovy Dressing (see page 264).

1 beef chuck shoulder roast,
    about 3 pounds
2 onions, peeled and sliced
3 tablespoons olive oil
2 garlic cloves, peeled
1 bay leaf
¼ cup minced fresh parsley
1 sprig fresh rosemary, or 1
    teaspoon dried rosemary,
    crumbled

1–2 fresh sage leaves, or ½
    teaspoon dried sage
    leaves, crumbled
Freshly ground pepper to taste
2 cups red wine vinegar
1 to 3 teaspoons sugar
1 cup dry white wine
2 cups water, or broth (see
    page 29)

Roast the meat, uncovered, in a preheated 325° oven for 1 to 1½ hours or until meat registers 140° on a meat thermometer. Meanwhile, sauté the onions in the oil in a large saucepan over low heat until they begin to color. Add the garlic, bay leaf, parsley, rosemary, sage, pepper, vinegar, and sugar. Simmer over low heat until the vinegar almost completely evaporates. Add the wine and water or broth. Bring to a boil, then turn down the heat so the liquid simmers for about 5 minutes. Reserve. Remove the strings from the meat if tied. Cut into ¼-inch-thick slices. Place slices overlapping in an earthenware, glass, or enamel dish with sides high enough to accommodate the marinade. Pour the hot marinade over the meat, cover, and refrigerate 1 full day or overnight. To serve, lift the meat from the marinade and arrange the slices on a platter. *Serves 6 to 8.*

POLPETTONE ALLA CAMPAGNOLA

beef and veal loaf

The loaf is nice, rustic fare but sophisticated in presentation.

1 cup loosely packed fresh
    bread without crusts
1 cup milk
1 pound ground beef
1 pound ground veal
¾ cup grated Parmesan
2 eggs, lightly beaten
Coarse salt and freshly ground
    pepper to taste
2 tablespoons all-purpose flour

1 tablespoon butter
3 tablespoons olive oil
1 bay leaf
1 sprig fresh thyme, or ¼
    teaspoon dried thyme
    leaves, crumbled
1 large sage leaf, fresh or
    dried
½ cup dry white wine
Caper Sauce (see page 269)

Soften the bread in the milk in a bowl for a few minutes. Squeeze dry and chop fine. Combine the ground beef, ground veal, grated Parmesan, and eggs with the bread. Season with salt and pepper and mix well. Shape into a sausage about 2½ inches thick. Roll in the flour to coat. Heat the butter and oil in a heavy-bottomed ovenproof casserole over medium heat. Gently put the meat in the pan, add the herbs, and transfer to a preheated 375° oven. Cook for 1 hour, carefully turning it every so often to brown all sides. Add the white wine a little at a time as needed. There should be a little moisture in the pan. When the meat is cooked, lift it out of the pan and let cool. Slice about ¼ inch thick. Arrange on a platter in overlapping slices. Spoon the Caper Sauce over. The meat can be cooked 1 or 2 days in advance. Wrap the unsliced loaf in plastic wrap or aluminum foil. Let come to room temperature before slicing. *Serves 6 to 8.*

VEAL ROAST FLAVORED WITH ROSEMARY AND GARLIC

Also delicious cooked with basil.

2 garlic cloves, peeled and
  minced
2 teaspoons minced fresh
  rosemary leaves, or 2
  teaspoons dried rosemary,
  crumbled, or 1 tablespoon
  minced fresh basil leaves,
  or 2 teaspoons dried basil
  leaves, crumbled

Coarse salt and freshly ground
  pepper to taste
1 boned veal loin, tied, about
  2 pounds
2 tablespoons olive oil
2 tablespoons butter
½ cup dry white wine, or as
  needed
Fruity olive oil

Make a paste with the garlic, rosemary or basil, salt, and pepper in a mortar and pestle, or crush with the flat side of a chef's knife. Make a few incisions with a sharp knife about ½ inch deep in the roast and stuff some of the paste into them. Rub remaining herb paste over the meat. Heat the olive oil and butter in a heavy-bottomed saucepan just large enough to hold the roast. When the foam subsides, add the veal and brown well on all sides. Add the wine. Cook at a very gentle simmer, partially covered, for about 45 minutes to 1 hour, adding more liquid if necessary. The meat is done when the juices run clear and a meat thermometer registers an internal temperature of 165°. Remove from the pan and let cool. Cut into thin slices and arrange on a platter. Season the meat with salt and pepper. Pour enough olive oil on the meat to lightly moisten it. *Serves 4 to 6.*

STUFFED VEAL BREAST

Stuffed meats may seem complicated to execute, but actually they only require the assembling of many ingredients. We recommend having everything measured and ready. The final assembly is quite simple and goes very quickly. This impressive looking dish is rich-tasting with ham, Parmesan and abundant parsley.

4 eggs, lightly beaten
1½ cups grated Parmesan cheese
½ pound ham, cut into small dice
1½ cups homemade bread crumbs
1¼ cups minced fresh parsley
Coarse salt and freshly ground pepper to taste
Ground nutmeg to taste

1 veal breast, about 6 pounds, boned with a pocket cut into it for stuffing
¼ cup olive oil
4 ounces pancetta, or blanched bacon, thickly sliced
1–2 cups dry white wine
4 sprigs fresh rosemary, or 1 tablespoon dried rosemary leaves, crumbled
2 sprigs fresh sage, or 4 dried sage leaves, crumbled

Combine the eggs, Parmesan, ham, bread crumbs, and parsley in a bowl. Season with the salt, pepper, and nutmeg. Fill the veal pocket with the stuffing. The breast will mound in the center. Sew up the opening with a needle and strong, white thread. Place the stuffed veal in a roasting pan. Rub 2 tablespoons of olive oil over one side of the veal. Season with salt and pepper. Turn the meat over and rub with the remaining olive oil. Season with salt and pepper. Place the pancetta over the top of meat. Roast in a preheated 350° oven for 15 minutes. Pour 1 cup of the wine over the meat. Scatter the herbs around the meat. Cook for an additional 2¼ hours. Baste occasionally and turn the meat over every once in a while to brown both sides. Add more wine if the pan becomes too dry. Remove the veal from the pan and let cool. Just before serving, cut the veal into ½-inch slices. *Serves 8.*

ARISTA
succulent pork roast with fennel

Arista is a Tuscan dish which is delicious served at room temperature. The roast, traditionally served with the bone in, has a particularly satisfying succulence because the darker meat of the loin infuses the leaner tenderloin with its juiciness. In this recipe, we use a boneless rib roast which allows for more thorough seasoning and easier slicing when serving.

6 garlic cloves, peeled and minced
1–2 tablespoons fennel seeds
2 teaspoons coarse salt

Freshly ground pepper to taste
1 boneless pork rib roast, about 4 pounds
Fruity olive oil

Make a paste with the minced garlic, fennel, salt and pepper in a mortar and pestle, or mash with the side of a chef's knife. If the roast is rolled and tied, unroll it. Spread most of the paste over the meat, reserving a tablespoon or so. Roll and tie the roast so that the white tenderloin is more or less in the center, surrounded by the darker meat of the loin. Make a few incisions with a sharp knife about ½ inch deep in the roast and stuff some of the paste into them. Rub any remaining paste over the outside of the meat. Rub a little olive oil over the meat and place in a roasting pan. Roast, uncovered, in a preheated 350° oven about 2 hours or until the internal temperature registers 170° on a meat thermometer. Baste the roast two or three times with the pan juices. Remove the roast from oven and allow to cool. When it is tepid, cut into ½-inch-thick slices and drizzle a little fruity olive oil over the meat if desired. Serve with Sage Potatoes (see page 165). *Serves 6 to 8.*

BAY-SCENTED PORK LIVER SPIEDINI

This unusual skewered meal has its origins in the Italian countryside where the rich flavor of strong meats and the aroma of sharp herbs are appreciated. The dish is especially distinctive in its abundant use of bay leaves. An assertive vegetable such as Kale with Black Olives (see page 152) is an appropriate complement.

1 large piece of caul fat
3 pounds pork livers
2 garlic cloves, peeled and put through press
1 tablespoon coarse salt
Freshly ground pepper to taste
1 day-old loaf good-quality Italian or French bread, crust removed and cut into 1½-inch cubes
24 bay leaves
Olive oil

Soak the caul fat in warm water for 30 minutes or until it is pliable. Divide the pork livers into 12 equal pieces, cutting out any tendons or other tough pieces. Drain the caul fat and dry with paper towels.

Cut it into 12 pieces large enough to wrap around the pork liver pieces. Mix together the garlic, salt, and pepper in a small dish. Rub the pieces of pork liver with the garlic mixture. Wrap each spiced piece of pork in a piece of caul fat. Set aside. Thread four metal skewers in the following manner. Start with 1 cube of bread, then 1 bay leaf, 1 piece of liver, bay leaf, bread, bay leaf, and continue so each skewer has 3 pieces of liver flanked with bay leaves. (If the bay leaves are too brittle to skewer, push them between the bread and liver.) Each skewer should begin and end with a bread cube. Generously brush the skewers with olive oil, making sure the bread is well oiled. Grill the skewers over hot coals or in a preheated hot broiler, turning occasionally until the livers are cooked through yet still slightly pink, about 15 to 20 minutes. Brush frequently with olive oil. Serve tepid—before it reaches room temperature. *Serves 4.*

GRILLED BUTTERFLIED LEG OF LAMB

A butterflied leg of lamb cooks more quickly and is easier to carve than a whole leg of lamb. However, the meat is of uneven thickness, so it is necessary to watch it carefully during cooking so that the thickest part of the meat is rare while the rest of the meat does not overcook. The lamb and rosemary with their aggressive flavors are well suited to each other in this simple, highly flavored dish.

1 leg of lamb, about 5 pounds, boned and butterflied
3 garlic cloves, peeled and minced
10–15 sprigs fresh rosemary, or 2 tablespoons dried rosemary leaves, crumbled
3–4 tablespoons olive oil
¼ cup strong Dijon or Moutard de Meaux (optional)
1 recipe Rosemary Vinaigrette (see page 264)

The night before cooking, rub the lamb well with the minced garlic, dried rosemary, and olive oil. If using fresh rosemary, place the herb in a bowl or baking dish and lay the lamb on top. Cover the meat tightly with plastic wrap and marinate overnight in the refrigerator. Let the meat come to room temperature before grilling. Lift the meat off the rosemary sprigs and rub all over with mustard. Place the lamb on a very hot grill. Turn every 15 minutes for a total cooking time of about 40 minutes for pink, and 1 hour for well-done meat. Pink or rare meat will register 160° on a meat thermometer, well done, 175°. Let the meat cool to room temperature before slicing. Cut into ½-inch-thick slices and arrange on a platter. Moisten lightly with the Rosemary Vinaigrette. Pass the extra dressing. *Serves 6 to 8.*

CHICKEN LIVER SPREAD WITH JUNIPER BERRIES

This highly flavored chicken liver pâté is a full-flavored addition to a cocktail buffet. It also makes a satisfying first course served with a chilled white wine. Juniper berries, most commonly associated with gin, lend their unique, richly aromatic flavor to this pâté. Serve on crostini (see page 9).

1 pound chicken livers
2 tablespoons butter
3 tablespoons olive oil
2 or 3 slices prosciutto, chopped
2 teaspoons minced fresh sage leaves, or ½ teaspoon dried sage leaves, crumbled
1 bay leaf

5 juniper berries, ground to a powder with mortar and pestle or in a small electric grinder
1 large garlic clove, peeled and minced
Coarse salt and freshly ground pepper to taste
1 tablespoon capers

Clean and chop the chicken livers. Melt the butter with the olive oil in a skillet over very low heat. Add the chicken livers, prosciutto, sage, bay leaf, juniper berries, garlic, salt, and pepper. Cook for about 10 minutes or just until cooked through. Let cool. Chop very finely with a chef's knife or in a food processor fitted with a steel blade by pulsing quickly. Turn into a small bowl. Garnish with capers. *Serves 6 to 8.*

ROSEMARY CHICKEN

This succulent chicken is redolent of rosemary and lemon. Placing the garlic under the skin subtly perfumes the meat. Served with a pasta dish and a green salad, the chicken is informal yet impressive, and supremely satisfying.

4 garlic cloves, peeled and crushed

1 large roasting chicken, about 4–5 pounds, washed and dried completely inside and out

4–5 fresh rosemary sprigs, or 1 tablespoon dried rosemary leaves, crumbled

1 lemon, halved

Coarse salt

Fresh rosemary sprigs and lemon wedges for garnish

Rub the garlic cloves over the outside of the bird and in the cavity. Slip 1 garlic clove between the flesh and skin of each breast and leave the remaining 2 inside the cavity. Rub the fresh or dried rosemary all over the bird. If using fresh rosemary, slip one sprig between the flesh and skin of each breast near the garlic. Place the remaining rosemary inside the cavity. Squeeze half the lemon into the cavity, the other over the outside of the bird. Discard 1 lemon half and place the other inside the cavity. Rub salt over the bird and in the cavity. Truss the chicken, if you desire. Place on a shallow rack, breast up, in a roasting pan. Roast in a preheated 400° oven for 1 to 1½ hours, basting once or twice, or until the juices run clear. Cool to room temperature. Carve into serving pieces and place on a platter. Garnish with rosemary sprigs and lemon wedges. *Serves 4 to 6.*

ORANGE-ROASTED CHICKEN WITH THYME

Honey basting gives the chicken a dressy sheen. Serve with Insalata di Riso Selvatico (see page 89).

1 large roasting chicken, about 4–5 pounds
1 garlic clove, peeled and crushed
1 bunch fresh thyme leaves, or 1 tablespoon dried thyme leaves, crumbled

2 oranges
Coarse salt and freshly ground pepper to taste
1 tablespoon honey
Fresh thyme sprigs and orange slices for garnish

Wash and dry the chicken completely inside and out. Trim excess fat. Rub the garlic clove over the outside of the bird and in the cavity. Leave it in the cavity. Rub the fresh or dried thyme all over the bird. If using fresh thyme, slip 1 or 2 sprigs between the flesh and skin of each breast. Stuff the cavity with the remaining thyme sprigs. Squeeze the juice of 1 orange over the outside of the chicken and inside the cavity. Place 1 orange half used for the juice in the cavity with the thyme sprigs. Rub salt and pepper over the outside of the bird and in the cavity. Cut the remaining orange into ¼-inch slices. Truss the chicken, placing 2 or 3 orange slices underneath the string over the breasts. Place the trussed chicken, breast up, on a rack in a shallow roasting pan. Roast in a preheated 400° oven for 1 to 1½ hours, basting frequently, or until the juices run clear. After 30 minutes of cooking time, mix the honey in the roasting pan with the hot juices. Serve barely warm or at room temperature, garnished with thyme sprigs and orange slices. *Serves 4 to 6.*

STUFFED BONED WHOLE CHICKEN

Ask your butcher to bone the chicken. He or she will no doubt do an excellent job and will save you from possible trauma. It is fun to assemble and cook this fascinating dish. It is elegant, yet has a definite rustic appeal, and makes perfect picnic food. Since the stuffing is dense, it keeps the chicken moist and flavorful. The skin turns a lovely golden brown. Handle the uncooked stuffed chicken carefully as it is a bit fragile at this stage and prone to tear. The finished chicken, however, is firm and easy to slice. But before you cut into it, let everyone see the stuffed chicken whole and marvel at it.

2 ounces fresh French or Italian bread, about 2 ½-inch slices
1 cup milk
2 sweet Italian sausages
¼ pound ham, diced
½ pound ground veal
½ cup grated Parmesan cheese
¼ cup chopped fresh parsley
1 egg, lightly beaten
Coarse salt and freshly ground pepper to taste

1 chicken, about 3½–4 pounds, boned, washed and dried completely inside and out, and excess fat trimmed
¼ cup olive oil
1 medium onion, peeled and coarsely chopped
1 garlic clove, peeled and coarsely chopped
3 bay leaves
½ cup brandy

Soften the bread in the milk in a small bowl for a few minutes until completely soft. Squeeze the bread to remove most of the milk.

Discard milk. Remove the casings from the sausage and crumble the meat. Combine the sausage meat, ham, veal, bread, Parmesan, parsley, egg, salt and pepper in a medium bowl. Mix well. Lay the chicken out flat, skin-side down. Spread the stuffing over the chicken, mounding it in the center. Fold over the sides of the chicken until they meet and sew closed with kitchen thread, leaving the stitches a little loose.

Carefully place the chicken on a rack in a shallow roasting pan. Rub with the olive oil and sprinkle generously with salt and pepper. Distribute the onion, garlic, and bay leaves around the chicken. Roast the chicken in a preheated 350° oven. After 15 minutes pour the brandy over the chicken. Continue cooking for about 1 hour, basting occasionally. Let cool completely. Slice and serve. Or wrap in plastic wrap and refrigerate for up to 2 days. Return to room temperature, slice, and serve. *Serves 6.*

ROLLED HERBED
CHICKEN BREASTS

Dried herbs work really well in this recipe. When the rolls of chicken are cut, the stuffing makes a lovely pinwheel design. We often serve this as an hors d'oeuvre at cocktail parties. Accompany with Basil Mayonnaise (see page 266).

4 whole chicken breasts, split, skinned, boned, and excess fat trimmed
4 cups fresh bread crumbs, lightly toasted
½ small onion, peeled and minced
1 garlic clove, peeled and minced or put through press
6 eggs, lightly beaten
Coarse salt and freshly ground pepper to taste
1 cup mixed fresh herbs, leaves minced (basil, thyme, rosemary, flat-leaf parsley, sage, and marjoram), or 1 teaspoon each dried sage and thyme leaves, crumbled, ½ teaspoon each dried basil and marjoram leaves, crumbled, and ¼ cup minced fresh parsley

Pound the chicken breasts between wax paper or plastic wrap to about ½ inch thickness. Mix together the bread crumbs, onion, garlic, eggs, salt, pepper, and herbs in a large bowl. Place the breasts smooth-side down. Place a generous tablespoon or so of the stuffing on each breast. Spread the stuffing so that it covers the breast. Roll the breast as you would an egg roll, tucking in the edges when possible. Place the rolled breasts close together in a lightly oiled baking dish. Lightly salt and pepper the rolls and cover with lightly oiled wax paper or parchment paper, cut to fit just inside the pan. Gently press the paper down so it rests directly on the rolls. Bake the chicken in a preheated 375° oven for 15 to 20 minutes or until the rolls are opaque and feel firm to the touch. Let the chicken cool in the refrigerator. To serve, cut the rolls into ¼-inch-thick slices so they look like pinwheels. Arrange on individual plates or on a serving platter. *Serves 4 to 6.*

POLLO TONNATO

chicken with tuna sauce and capers

This is a variation on the famous vitello tonnato, veal with tuna sauce. Our version is inspired by a cookbook from 1907 written by Pellegrino Artusi. The tuna sauce does not contain mayonnaise, which is usually found in modern recipes; it is lighter, less rich. A great dish for entertaining, it can be made well in advance. Just arrange on a platter, wrap tightly in plastic wrap, and refrigerate until needed. You can also use a whole poached chicken instead of chicken breasts. Poach the chicken with aromatic vegetables, remove the skin and bones, and cut the meat into neat pieces. Garnish with various condiments such as olives or cornichons, but we lean toward simplicity, using only large capers and lemon slices.

FOR THE CHICKEN:

1 carrot, peeled and thinly sliced
1 celery stalk, thinly sliced
½ medium onion, peeled and thinly sliced

3 tablespoons olive oil
½ cup dry white wine
3 whole chicken breasts, split, skinned, boned, and excess fat trimmed

Use a skillet just large enough to hold the chicken breasts in 1 layer. Sauté the sliced vegetables in the oil in the skillet, covered, over low heat until the vegetables are wilted, about 10 minutes. Add the wine and cook another 2 minutes. Add the chicken breasts, cover, and cook for 10 to 15 minutes, depending on thickness of chicken breasts. Let cool in the broth.

FOR THE SAUCE:

1 can (7 ounces) chunk light
   tuna in oil, drained
½ cup olive oil
4 tablespoons lemon juice

6 canned flat anchovies
1 tablespoon capers
Coarse salt (optional)

Combine the tuna, olive oil, lemon juice, and anchovies in a blender. Blend until smooth and light colored. Stir in the capers. Add salt if necessary.

TO ASSEMBLE THE DISH:
Capers
Thin lemon slices

Cut the chicken breasts into ¼-inch-thick scallops. Spread a little of the tuna sauce on a platter. Place the chicken scallops on top of the sauce. Cover with the remaining sauce. Wrap tightly in plastic wrap. Refrigerate. To serve, garnish with capers and thin lemon slices. *Serves 4 to 6.*

CHICKEN BREASTS POACHED IN ORANGE JUICE AND SAGE

Poached in orange juice, the chicken flesh is moist and silky. Garnish with orange slices and serve with Cranberry-Mint Relish (see page 281) for an especially pretty luncheon presentation.

*Coarse salt and freshly ground
   pepper to taste*
*4 whole chicken breasts,
   skinned, split, boned, and
   excess fat trimmed*
*1 bunch fresh sage leaves, or 1
   tablespoon dried sage
   leaves, crumbled*

½ cup fresh orange juice
2 navel oranges
*Fresh sage leaves or parsley
   for garnish*

Lightly salt and pepper the chicken breasts and lay them side by side in a lightly oiled roasting pan. Place a pinch of dry sage or 1 fresh sage leaf underneath and on top of each breast. Pour the orange juice over chicken. Cover with lightly oiled wax paper or parchment paper cut to fit just inside the pan so it rests directly on the chicken. Poach the breasts in a preheated 375° oven for 8 to 10 minutes or until the flesh is opaque and feels firm to the touch. Cool the chicken in the pan. Meanwhile, slice the oranges crosswise into thin slices, then halve these slices. Either present the chicken breasts whole, garnished with the orange slices, or cut each breast crosswise into 4 pieces, and arrange them on individual plates alternately with an orange half moon. Decorate with fresh sage or parsley. *Serves 4 to 6.*

CHICKEN IN BALSAMIC VINEGAR

This is an elegant way to prepare chicken that combines the subtle sweetness of balsamic vinegar with raisins and lemon zest. It must be made 24 hours in advance to allow the flavors to penetrate the chicken. Balsamic vinegar is made in Modena, Italy, according to ancient, secret recipes. Because of its full-bodied taste, it is often used with meats in place of meat stock. It should not be used as an all-purpose vinegar, but discreetly where its special qualities are called for. Here it is paired with the delicate flavor of the chicken. Serve on arugola leaves; their pungency adds to the intriguing blend of flavors. If arugola is not available, tender spinach leaves will work very well.

4 whole chicken breasts,
skinned, split, boned, and
fat trimmed
Coarse salt and freshly ground
pepper to taste
½ cup fruity white wine, or
water
¼ cup plus 2 tablespoons
balsamic vinegar
¾ cup fruity olive oil

4 sprigs fresh tarragon, or 1
teaspoon dried tarragon
leaves, crumbled
Zest of 1 small lemon,
removed with a vegetable
peeler
4 tablespoons raisins, plumped
in hot water for 15
minutes and drained
Arugola leaves for garnish

Slightly flatten the chicken breasts with the palm of your hand. Place in a lightly oiled, shallow roasting pan. Lightly salt and pepper. Add the wine or water to the pan. Cover with lightly oiled parchment paper or wax paper cut to just fit the pan. Bake in a preheated 375° oven for about 10 minutes or until cooked through. Let the chicken cool in the pan.

Whisk together the vinegar and olive oil in a bowl. Add the tarragon, lemon zest, and raisins. Arrange the chicken breasts in 1 layer in a shallow dish just large enough to hold them. Pour the dressing over the chicken. Cover with plastic wrap and marinate in the refrigerator at least 12 hours, turning the chicken occasionally. Before serving, return to room temperature. Place the arugola leaves on individual plates or on a platter and arrange the chicken on the leaves. Garnish with the raisins and lemon zest, and drizzle a little of the marinade over the chicken. *Serves 4 to 6.*

HERB CHICKEN CUTLETS

The chicken breasts are breaded and cooked quickly in hot oil to seal in all the juices. They come out crusty and golden. Drain well to keep crisp. These are perfect to take along on a picnic. As an alternative to the lemon wedges, serve with Lemon Mayonnaise (see page 265) or another flavored mayonnaise.

*2 whole chicken breasts,
    skinned, split, boned, and
    excess fat trimmed*
2 eggs
1 cup bread crumbs
*2 teaspoons minced fresh
    rosemary leaves*

*Coarse salt and freshly ground
    pepper to taste*
Olive oil
Lemon wedges

Gently pound the chicken flat between pieces of wax paper or plastic wrap. Butterfly the thick areas by cutting into the flesh horizontally. Lightly beat the eggs in a shallow bowl. Combine the bread crumbs and rosemary in a small bowl. Season with salt and pepper and spread the bread crumbs on a plate. Dip the chicken in the egg and then in the bread crumbs, coating both sides. Pat the meat to help the crumbs adhere. Pour enough olive oil into a skillet to come to a depth of ⅜ inch. When the oil is sizzling hot, fry the breaded chicken until golden brown on both sides, about 4 minutes. Place the chicken on paper towels to drain and season with salt and pepper. Serve the cutlets with lemon wedges on the side. *Serves 4.*

GRILLED CHICKEN LEGS WITH OREGANO, LEMON, AND BLACK PEPPER

Good on a picnic. These taste best if grilled on a barbecue using natural wood coals such as mesquite, but they can be done successfully in a broiler.

6 whole chicken legs
½ cup olive oil
¼ cup lemon juice

*2 teaspoons dried oregano
leaves, crumbled*
*Coarse salt and freshly ground
pepper to taste*

Wash the chicken and dry completely. Trim excess fat. Combine the olive oil, lemon juice, oregano, and a generous amount of coarsely ground pepper in a small bowl. Beat lightly with a fork. Place the chicken in a shallow dish and brush with the sauce. Cover with plastic wrap and marinate for 2 hours or as long as overnight in the refrigerator. Remove the chicken from marinade, salt, and place on a hot grill or in a preheated broiler. Turn the chicken legs over several times while cooking and brush with the marinade. Cook about 35 minutes or until the juices run clear. Let cool and serve at room temperature. *Serves 6.*

TURKEY BREAST WITH HERB BUTTER

Turkey breast has a fine, delicate flavor and texture akin to veal. Cooking it tightly wrapped in foil seals in all the juices and protects against dryness. To serve, slice and arrange in an overlapping pattern for a simple but elegant presentation.

4 tablespoons softened butter
1 tablespoon minced fresh rosemary leaves, or 1 tablespoon dried rosemary leaves, crumbled
1 tablespoon minced fresh sage leaves, or 1 teaspoon dried sage leaves, crumbled
1 tablespoon minced fresh parsley
Coarse salt and freshly ground pepper to taste
1 small turkey breast or ½ large turkey breast, about 3 pounds, skinned, boned, and butterflied

Work together the softened butter, herbs, salt, and pepper in a small bowl with a wooden spoon until the herbs are well incorporated. Spread the turkey breast out, smooth-side down, in a flat piece. Season with salt and pepper. Spread all but about 1 tablespoon of herb butter over the turkey. Roll up tightly in a sausage shape and tie like a roast. Place the turkey on a sheet of aluminum foil. Season the outside of the roll with salt and pepper and rub with the remaining herb butter. Wrap tightly in the foil. Place on a baking sheet and cook in a preheated 400° oven for about 50 minutes. Be careful not to overcook. Remove from the oven and let cool in the foil. Slice just before serving. *Serves 6.*

THYME-SCENTED QUAIL

The brandy infuses the quail with its strong, fragrant bouquet. Serve with Grilled Stuffed Wild Mushrooms (see page 158) and Wild and White Rice Salad (see page 88).

10–12 quail (2 per person)
Coarse salt and freshly ground
pepper to taste
1 bunch fresh thyme sprigs, or
1 tablespoon dried thyme
leaves, crumbled

2 tablespoons minced fresh
flat-leaf parsley
3 garlic cloves, peeled and
coarsely chopped
1 cup brandy
¼ pound bacon, sliced
Fresh thyme sprigs for garnish

Cut each quail through the breastbone with a sharp knife or poultry shears so that it lies flat. Salt and pepper generously. Place in a glass or enamel pan, overlapping as little as possible. Sprinkle with thyme, parsley, and garlic. Pour brandy over. Cover and marinate at least 3 hours. The longer they marinate, the stronger the flavor.

Blanch the bacon in boiling water about 2 minutes. Drain, cool under cold water, and pat dry with paper towels.

Lift the quail from the marinade, reserving the liquid. Place the quail in a shallow baking pan and cover with the blanched bacon to prevent them from drying out. Roast in a preheated 400° oven for about 10 minutes, basting frequently with the reserved marinade. Meanwhile, strain the remaining marinade and put in a saucepan over medium heat to reduce by one-third. When the quail are done, remove from the oven, discard the bacon, and arrange on a platter. Decorate with fresh thyme sprigs and pass the reduced marinade. Serve at room temperature. *Serves 4 to 6.*

fruit desserts

CHERRIES POACHED IN CHIANTI

On a train bound for Zurich, we saw cherry trees with ripe red cherries dangling like earrings from the branches. Since cherries and almonds are a classic combination, we suggest serving Italian almond cookies with this rich dessert.

A cherry pitter is one of those stocking-stuffer gadgets that turn out to be quite useful, not only for pitting cherries but also for pitting olives. If you do not have one handy, do not despair. Cut into the cherry without cutting it in half and pluck out the pit. Vary the amount of sugar, depending on the sweetness of the cherries.

CONTINUED

2 pounds cherries, pitted
½–1 cup sugar

2 cups rich Chianti, or other
full-bodied red wine

Put the cherries in a saucepan. Add the sugar and wine. Stir to combine. Bring to a boil. Lower the heat to a simmer and cook for about 10 minutes. Remove the cherries from the poaching liquid with a slotted spoon. Place in a bowl. Reduce the liquid until it is thick and syrupy. Pour over the cherries. Chill in the refrigerator until ready to serve. *Serves 6.*

CANTALOUPE WITH ANISETTE

One of the most refreshing ways to end a meal. Select a fragrant cantaloupe that yields to gentle pressure at the stem end.

1 large cantaloupe
¼ cup anisette

2 tablespoons water

Trim away with a knife the peel and any green areas from the cantaloupe. Cut the cantaloupe in half and scoop out the seeds. Cut into crescents about ¾ inch thick. Arrange in 1 layer in a glass or enamel dish. Combine the anisette and water and pour over the melon. Cover with plastic wrap and refrigerate for 1 to 4 hours. Lift the melon out of the liquid and arrange on a platter. Serve chilled. *Serves 4.*

MELE RIPIENE CON PIGNOLI

apples stuffed with pine nuts

Serve these at the end of a rustic dinner or as part of a brunch. They're good, homey fare. The sweetness depends on the natural flavor of the apple. The nuts add a creamy texture and a subtle flavor.

¼ *cup raisins*	*4 cooking apples*
¼ *cup pine nuts*	*2 tablespoons butter*
½ *teaspoon grated lemon zest*	¾ *cup dry white, or red wine*
¼ *cup sugar*	*Crème fraîche, or heavy cream (optional)*

Soak the raisins in boiling water to cover in a small bowl for 15 minutes. Drain. Combine with the pine nuts, lemon zest, and sugar in a small bowl. Core the apples without cutting all the way through. Peel the apples one-third of the way down from the top. Stuff with the raisin-nut mixture. Place the apples in a buttered medium baking dish and cover each with thin shavings of butter. Pour the wine over apples. Bake in a preheated 400° oven for 25 minutes to 1 hour, depending on the size and firmness of the apples. Baste every 15 minutes or so, until the apples are tender but not mushy. Serve plain, or with crème fraîche or heavy cream. *Serves 4.*

BUYING FRESH FIGS

A ripe fig is intensely sweet with a luscious, jam-like texture. Because they are very fragile when ripe, commercial figs are picked unripe and often fall short of their promise. Finding a source for tree-ripened figs would naturally be the ideal solution. Lacking that, carefully select figs that are extremely soft and yield very easily to pressure. A perfectly ripe fig, and there are few things better, will be slightly withered at the stem and have splits in the skin. As the Italian saying goes, a ripe fig should have "Il collo d'impiccato e la camicia da furfante"; or roughly translated, a neck like a man who has been hanged and an open shirt like that worn by a thief. Figs come in a range of colors depending on the variety, from delicate shades of yellow and green, to dusky brown and purple, to black.

CARAMELIZED FIGS

Eating figs evokes an interweaving of memories—during childhood, lazily eating figs from a neighbor's tree during a hot Los Angeles summer; sitting beside the Mediterranean under an arbor of grapevines and being presented with a plate of ripe, glistening figs to be eaten with the fingers.

12 or more ripe fresh green or   *¼ cup sugar*
       black figs   *1 cup whipped cream*

Carefully wipe the figs clean. Cut them lengthwise in half through the stem. Place them cut-side up in a baking dish. Sprinkle generously with sugar. Bake in a preheated 400° oven for 7 to 10 minutes or until the sugar has browned. Let cool and serve with whipped cream on the side. *Serves 6 to 8.*

FIGS POACHED IN RED WINE

This rich and succulent dessert is a good way to treat less than perfectly sweet figs.

1 liter deep red wine, such as Barolo or Barbera
2–3 cups sugar

16 purple figs, yielding but not soft

Combine the wine and sugar in a large saucepan or skillet with high sides. Bring to boil over medium heat. Cover and cook 5 minutes or until the sugar completely dissolves. Lower the heat so the syrup simmers. Gently lower the figs into the syrup. Cook until the figs are imbued with the syrup and tender, about 8 minutes. Lift the figs from the syrup with a slotted spoon onto a serving platter. Bring the wine syrup back to a boil and cook until it reduces to a thick, syrupy consistency. Pour over the figs. Let cool. Serve with slightly sweetened whipped cream or Red Wine Granita with Thyme (see page 257). *Serves 8.*

BLACK GRAPES IN PORT

Black grapes do have seeds. If you prefer, you can cut the grapes in half around the middle without cutting all the way through, twist the two halves apart, and remove the seeds. Proceed as directed in the recipe, but reduce the marinating time to 2 to 3 hours. But we like the way the grapes with seeds encourage lingering at the table. A mood is created that is conducive to conversation and relaxation.

1 pound black grapes, in
bunches
3 cups rich ruby port or
enough to cover the grapes

6 thick strips lemon peel
Ice cubes

Place the grapes in a bowl. Cover with the port. Add the lemon peel. Cover tightly with plastic wrap and let marinate overnight. To serve, lift the grapes out of the port. Cut into clusters and arrange in a shallow bowl with ice cubes. The port can be strained and reused. *Serves 4.*

C A R A M E L I Z E D   O R A N G E S

A combination of navel and red blood oranges makes this dessert a spectacular presentation.

8 seedless navel and/or blood
oranges
3 cups sugar

1 cup plus 2 tablespoons water
Pinch cream of tartar

Make long, thin strips of peel from 2 oranges with a one-holed lemon stripper. Peel the oranges with a sharp knife, removing all the white pith. Cut a small slice from the bottom of each to make the oranges stand upright. Blanch the strips of orange peel in boiling water for 5 minutes. Drain in a sieve and refresh under cold running water.

Combine the sugar, water, and cream of tartar in a small, heavy saucepan. Bring to a boil over medium heat. Cover and boil 5 minutes or until the sugar syrup is transparent. Uncover and continue cooking until the syrup registers 250° on a candy thermometer or until a spoonful poured into a glass of cold water turns into a hard ball. Lower the heat. Using a long meat fork, dip each orange into the syrup so that it is covered. Lift out and onto a serving dish.

After the oranges are candied, cook the strips of orange peel in the remaining syrup for about 5 minutes. Remove the peel, separating the strands, and place on oiled wax paper. When the strips of peel are hard and cool, use them to decorate the oranges. Oranges can be sliced or quartered before dipping, but first let them drain on paper towels for at least 1 hour. *Serves 8.*

P E A C H E S   I N   R E D   W I N E

Peaches and red wine have an amazing affinity for each other, one imparting its own subtle flavor to the other. The peaches stain a beautiful, deep, ruby red, and the wine tastes perfumed by the peaches. Finding intensely sweet, perfumed peaches is a challenge in this day and age, for they have suffered much at the hands of modern agriculture. When selecting peaches, pick those that are fragrant and allow them to ripen fully before using. The flesh should yield to gentle pressure.

8 medium peaches
1 liter bottle dry light red
    wine

½ cup sugar
1 cinnamon stick

Dip the peaches in boiling water for several seconds. Peel. Cut the peaches in half along the natural line of the fruit and remove the pits. Combine the red wine and sugar in a saucepan. Stir over low heat until the sugar melts. Place the peaches in glass bowl and pour the wine over them so that it completely covers the peaches. Add the cinnamon stick. Cover the bowl with plastic wrap and refrigerate for 3 days. Remove the peaches from the wine and serve very cold along with a glass of the peach-flavored wine. *Serves 8.*

COPPA DI PESCHE

peaches with amaretti, marsala, and whipped cream

A dessert in the style of those wonderful, baroque creations served at outdoor cafes all over Italy, where a magnificent array of fruits, ice cream, and liqueurs are layered in huge, glass goblets. We offer our version with poached peaches and Marsala-soaked amaretti topped with a flourish of whipped cream.

4 large firm ripe peaches
1 cup water
½ cup sugar
Juice of ½ lemon

12 amaretti cookies
¼ cup dry Marsala
Whipped cream

Dip the peaches in boiling water for several seconds. Peel. Cut the peaches in half along the natural line of the fruit and remove the pits. Put peaches in a saucepan. Add the water, sugar, and lemon juice. Bring to a boil. Lower the heat and simmer until the peaches are just tender. Let the peaches cool in the liquid. Put 3 amaretti cookies in each of the 4 dessert goblets. Moisten the amaretti with the Marsala. Place two peach halves on the amaretti and top with whipped cream. *Serves 4.*

PEACHES STUFFED WITH AMARETTI, ALMONDS, AND CHOCOLATE

Serve chilled or at room temperature. The filling forms a crisp surface that contrasts with the smooth flesh of the peaches. These can be made a day in advance.

2 ounces amaretti cookies
¼ cup blanched almonds
3 tablespoons rum
¼ cup sugar

1 teaspoon unsweetened cocoa
*   powder*
1 egg yolk
4 large firm ripe peaches
1 tablespoon butter

Crush the amaretti and almonds to a fine crumb in a blender, food processor, or with a mortar and pestle. Transfer to a small mixing bowl. Add the rum, sugar, unsweetened cocoa, and egg yolk. Mix thoroughly. Cut the peaches in half along the natural line of the fruit.

Remove the pits. Scoop out a little of the peach flesh to enlarge the cavity. Finely chop the scooped-out flesh and add to the amaretti mixture. Spoon a little of the filling into each peach half. Top with thin shavings of butter and place the halves in a buttered baking dish. Bake at 350° for 45 minutes or until the filling firms up and forms a crust. Let cool. Transfer to a serving dish. *Serves 4.*

PEACHES WITH ZABAGLIONE-FLAVORED WHIPPED CREAM

The flavored whipped cream is equally good over sliced and sugared strawberries. If necessary, sprinkle sugar to taste on the sliced peaches.

6 large firm ripe peaches
3 eggs, separated
5 tablespoons sugar

3 tablespoons dry Marsala
1 cup whipping cream

Dip the peaches in boiling water for several seconds. Peel. Cut in half along the natural line of the fruit and remove the pits. Cut into thin slices. Combine the egg yolks and 3 tablespoons of the sugar in the top of a double boiler or in a small bowl. Beat until foamy and light in color. Slowly stir in the Marsala. Place over simmering water. Stir continuously until the mixture thickens. As soon as it thickens, remove from the heat. Keep stirring for a bit off the heat, and stir occasionally as it cools. Beat the cream with the remaining sugar in a small bowl until very stiff. Swirl the zabaglione into the whipped cream, leaving streaks. Place the sliced peaches in 6 dessert goblets. Cover the peaches with the zabaglione-flavored whipped cream. *Serves 6.*

PEARS WITH GORGONZOLA AND GOAT CHEESE

A rich, winter dessert.

¼ pound gorgonzola
¼ pound goat cheese
2 tablespoons heavy cream

4 firm ripe crisp pears
Juice of 1 lemon
¼ cup chopped walnuts

Place the gorgonzola, goat cheese, and cream in a bowl. Blend together with a fork. Cut the pears in half and core. Do not peel. Sprinkle the cut surfaces with lemon juice to prevent discoloration. Place the cheese mixture into a pastry bag fitted with a simple rosette tip. Pipe the cheese onto the cut side of each pear in a thick strip down the middle. Sprinkle the cheese with the walnuts. *Serves 4 to 6.*

FRESH ITALIAN PRUNES IN PORT

Italian prunes are a delicious variety of plum often overlooked. The deep yellow flesh becomes tinted by the ruby red color of the port. Serve as a compote or as a topping for vanilla ice cream.

1½ pounds Italian prunes
2 cups sugar
2 cups port

Pinch ground allspice
Pinch ground cloves

Cut the prunes lengthwise with a paring knife around the pit. Twist the halves apart and remove the pit. Cut the prunes lengthwise into quarters. Combine the sugar and port in a medium saucepan. Bring to a boil. Add the spices and prunes and bring back to a boil. Lower the heat and simmer until the prunes are tender, about 15 minutes. Lift the prunes with a slotted spoon out of the poaching liquid and place in a bowl. Boil the remaining liquid over high heat until it thickens slightly and reduces by one-quarter. Pour the liquid over the prunes and chill. *Serves 6.*

THE MAESTRO'S BERRIES

A friend of ours, a composer and record producer, makes a ritual of this preparation. The combination of the sweet and sour flavors of the balsamic vinegar and sugar enhances the flavor of the strawberries. This is an excellent way to serve berries that are not quite as sweet as they could be. Strawberries are also delicious served simply in a bowl with a drizzle of balsamic vinegar over them.

Strawberries, washed and
        with stem on

Sugar

Balsamic vinegar

Let the strawberries dry and arrange in a serving bowl. Supply each guest with a small dessert plate. Pour about 1 tablespoon of sugar on each plate. Pour just enough balsamic vinegar, about 2 teaspoons, over the mound of sugar so that a paste forms. Dip the strawberries into sugar-vinegar paste and eat. Serve with strong espresso.

S T R A W B E R R I E S   I N   R E D   W I N E

One of the finest ways to end a meal that we know. A match made in food heaven. Marsala can also be used in place of the red wine.

2 baskets strawberries
2 cups dry red wine, or dry
        Marsala

½ cup sugar or to taste

Cut out the stem of the strawberries with a paring knife. Cut the strawberries in half or in quarters, and put in a large bowl. Add the red wine and sugar. Gently mix to combine the ingredients. Cover and refrigerate for several hours before serving. *Serves 4.*

GELO DI MELONE
watermelon gel

This beautiful dessert has an intense, sweet flavor. It is served in restaurants all over Palermo. Serve small portions of the pink-colored gel in dessert goblets.

2–3 pounds watermelon, or
    enough to make 2 cups
    juice
¼ cup sugar
3 tablespoons cornstarch

2 ounces bitter-sweet
    chocolate, slivered
3 tablespoons unsalted
    pistachios, skinned and
    coarsely chopped
Pinch ground cinnamon

Remove the rind from the watermelon and cut the fruit into chunks. Put through a food mill or press through a sieve to get 2 cups of liquid without seeds. Combine the watermelon juice, sugar, and cornstarch in a saucepan, and stir until the cornstarch is completely dissolved. Bring to a boil and let cook for 4 to 5 minutes, stirring constantly, or until the mixture thickens. Let cool. Add the chocolate slivers and stir. Refrigerate until very cold. Spoon into dessert goblets. Garnish with chopped pistachios and dust with cinnamon. _Serves 6._

WATERMELON AND WINE

We first experienced Watermelon and Wine on a country picnic in Tuscany. A rather sweet red wine was used. Consultation with food and wine writer Colman Andrews yielded a lighter, more refreshing, and more drinkable suggestion.

1 medium ripe watermelon,
preferably round instead
of oval

1 liter bottle soft California
Chenin Blanc, such as
Charles Krug

Cut off a slice from one end of the watermelon, creating a lid. Carefully cut out the core of the fruit which has all the seeds. Fill the cavity with the wine. Remove the mature black seeds from the watermelon core and cut the fruit into slices. Refill the wine-soaked cavity with the sliced fruit. Replace the top and seal the incision with melted wax, using a burning candle. Place the watermelon in the refrigerator or in a large ice bucket, lid-side up, or in a portable cooler if picnic bound. To serve, remove the wax, lift the lid, and strain the wine through cheesecloth into a decanter or pitcher. Serve the watermelon slices accompanied by glasses of the watermelon wine. *Serves 10 to 12.*

MASCARPONE WITH RUM-SOAKED RAISINS

A fresh-tasting dessert to serve during winter months.

½ cup golden raisins
Dark rum
5 teaspoons sugar

1 pound mascarpone (see
page 91)
½ cup whipping cream

Place the raisins in a small bowl and add enough rum to cover. Let macerate at least 1 hour. Strain, reserving the rum. Beat together the sugar, mascarpone, and reserved rum in a bowl with a whisk or wooden spoon. Beat the whipping cream in a separate bowl until it forms soft peaks. Gently fold raisins and whipped cream into the mascarpone. Spoon into individual dessert cups and chill at least 1 hour before serving. *Serves 4 to 6.*

MASCARPONE WITH RASPBERRY PURÉE

The sweet berry flavor merges with the creamy mascarpone to create a lovely dish which is the essence of summertime.

½ pound raspberries
1 pound mascarpone (see
page 91)

5 teaspoons sugar
½ teaspoon vanilla

Try to avoid washing the raspberries if possible. Set aside a few berries to use as garnish and purée the rest in a blender or food processor. Strain the purée into a small bowl to remove the seeds. Beat together the mascarpone, sugar, vanilla, and raspberry purée with an electric mixer until smooth and fluffy. Spoon into individual dessert cups and garnish with whole raspberries. Refrigerate at least 1 hour before serving. *Serves 4 to 6.*

RISO E FRUTTA
mixed fruits with rice

An unusual combination of fresh fruits and rice. Any kind of rice works well here, but the short-grained arborio works especially well. Make sure the rice is cooked al dente by testing it frequently. If overcooked, it will become mushy after it marinates in the fruit juices. Serve in glass goblets to show off the contrasting fruit colors and the fruit-stained rice.

⅔ cup raw rice, preferably
   short-grain arborio
½ basket strawberries
2 large nectarines
3 plums

2 kiwis
Juice of 2 oranges
Juice of ½ lemon
½ cup sugar

Cook the rice in an abundant amount of boiling salted water in a large saucepan until al dente, still firm and with the slightest "bite" to it. Drain in a colander and run under cold water to stop further cooking. Let drain in the colander until dry. Hull the strawberries and cut into small dice. Cut the nectarines in half along the natural line of the fruit. Remove the pits. Place the halves cut-side down, cut into thin slices, and dice. Cut the plums in the same way as the nectarines. Peel the kiwis with a paring knife. Cut into a dice. Combine the rice with the diced fruit, orange juice, lemon juice, and sugar in a bowl. Toss well to mix. Chill about 1 hour before serving. *Serves 4.*

RICOTTA AND
CRYSTALLIZED HONEY

In Italy ricotta is a perfect example of a poverty food elevated to the sublime. There it is made from the whey left from the making of Pecorino, a sheep's milk cheese. American ricotta is made of milk, either skimmed or whole, and its texture is soft rather than the firm, cake-like texture of the Italian. For this dish the firm texture of the true Ricotta Romana is desired so that the ricotta may be cut into slices. It is therefore necessary to weight the American ricotta and let the excess moisture drain away. We had this simple dish for dessert at a Milanese restaurant, Ciovassino, where it was presented in tiny terra cotta bowls which contrasted beautifully with the white of the cheese.

2 pounds ricotta
½ cup almonds, coarsely
  chopped

Crystallized honey (miele
  amaro)

If you are unable to find firm Italian ricotta, you must drain your American ricotta of excess moisture. Line a colander or a heart-shaped coeur à la creme basket with a double thickness of cheesecloth. Place the ricotta in the colander or basket, cover with cheesecloth, and place a small heavy can on top to weight down the cheese. Stand the colander or basket on a plate to catch the whey and place it all in the refrigerator overnight. Place the almonds in a pie tin and roast in a preheated 375° oven for 5 minutes or until lightly browned.

To serve, unmold the ricotta. Carefully cut with a sharp knife into thin slices. Cut slices in half diagonally, forming small triangles. Arrange 4 triangles on a small dessert plate; servings should be small as this dish is *very* filling. Place 1 teaspoon of crystallized honey on top of the ricotta. Sprinkle roasted almonds on top of the honey. Serve with a demitasse spoon. *Serves 8 to 10.*

RED WINE GRANITA WITH THYME

Egg whites are not added to a granita, which is what gives it its characteristically coarse-grained texture. The simplest of frozen desserts, it is made of iced sugar syrup with a fruit purée or other flavoring, in this case a rich red wine.

3 cups red wine
1 cup water
½–¾ cup sugar

4 sprigs fresh thyme, or 1
*   teaspoon dried thyme*
*   leaves*
Fresh thyme sprigs for garnish
*   (optional)*

Combine the wine, water, sugar, and thyme in a heavy enamel or stainless steel saucepan. Bring to a boil over moderate heat. Cover and cook until the sugar dissolves, about 5 minutes. Strain out the thyme and pour the syrup into shallow metal baking pans or ice cube trays. Freeze until firm but not hard. Beat the ice in a food processor fitted with a steel blade, until smooth. Put the mixture back into the trays and freeze again until just firm. Scoop the granita into small chilled bowls and garnish with thyme sprigs. Serve with the Figs Poached in Red Wine (see page 243), if you wish. *Serves 8.*

TEA GRANITA AND PEACHES STEEPED IN COGNAC

This dessert might be served in an elegant Milanese sidewalk cafe.

4 cups strong hot tea, sugared to taste and cooled
2 large firm ripe peaches

½ cup Cognac
2–3 tablespoons sugar

Pour the tea into a shallow metal baking pan or into ice cube trays. Place in the freezer and stir occasionally as ice crystals form. Dip the peaches in boiling water. Peel. Cut in half along the natural line of the fruit and remove the pits. Cut into slices. Place in a bowl along with the Cognac and sugar and marinate for up to 1 hour in the refrigerator. The granita is ready when all the liquid has frozen into a soft mass of ice crystals. Serve in chilled dessert goblets garnished with the marinated peaches and Cognac. *Serves 4.*

ESPRESSO JELLY

A fun, trompe l'oeil dessert. In Japan coffee jelly is served unsweetened with sugar syrup on the side.

2 cups freshly brewed strong espresso
Sugar to taste
1 envelope (1 tablespoon) unflavored gelatin

Whipped cream sweetened with sugar to taste
Chocolate-covered coffee beans for garnish

Add sugar to taste to hot espresso, remembering that it will taste less sweet when chilled. Pour gelatin into a small bowl. Add hot sweetened espresso. Stir until the gelatin dissolves completely. Pour into espresso cups. Place in refrigerator and chill until the jelly becomes firm, about 2 hours. Before serving, garnish the jelly with a mound of whipped cream topped with chocolate-covered coffee beans. Serve with rolled wafer cookies, café style. *Note:* To fill 6 parfait glasses, double the amounts. *Serves 6.*

BISCOTTI AND VIN SANTO

Italian almond cookies, Biscotti di prato, or anise cookies, anicini, served with a dessert wine are a fitting end to a rustic meal. The firm, dry cookies are dipped into small, plain, stemless glasses of wine and then eaten accompanied by small sips of the wine. The wine-soaked cookie is moist yet still crunchy. We love the elemental ritual of dipping cookies in wine. It releases the child in us. Use a sweet dessert wine, preferably Vin Santo, but other fortified wines such as Marsala or port will work well. Biscotti and Vin Santo is the adult equivalent of cookies and milk.

1 bottle sweet dessert wine   *2 dozen Italian almond or*
                                       anise cookies

Pour the wine into low, stemless glasses. Offer a basket of the cookies to dip into wine. *Serves 6.*

dressings and condiments

The variety of flavors possible with oils and herbs and spices is practically infinite. These are two simple but delicious and useful aromatic oils. Once you get into the habit of making an herbed oil every month or so you will tend to actually use them and not have them just to decorate your kitchen shelves. We use rosemary oil most frequently and therefore include these two recipes. We suggest you experiment with your favorite herbs to produce a flavored oil to suit your taste.

OLIVE OIL WITH ROSEMARY AND GARLIC

8 fresh rosemary sprigs
2 garlic cloves, peeled and
   minced
1 level teaspoon coarse salt

2 black peppercorns
2 cups fruity olive oil

Clean the rosemary well with a damp cloth, being careful not to let the herb become damp. Detach the small, spiky leaves and discard the woody twigs and stems. Finely mince the rosemary leaves. Place the rosemary with the garlic, coarse salt, and black peppercorns in a sterilized pint glass jar. Cover with olive oil and seal. Keep in a cool place. Use for salads and cooking. Adds flavor to pasta dishes. *Makes 1 pint.*

ROSEMARY OIL

2 or 3 fresh sprigs rosemary
1 bottle fruity olive oil

Clean the rosemary well with a damp cloth, being careful not to let the herb become damp. Dry with paper towels. Pour out 1 or 2 tablespoons of oil from the bottle. Add the rosemary, seal, and let steep in a cool place for 2 months. Wonderful served on grilled meats.

SIMPLE VIRGIN DRESSING

In Europe this type of dressing is most often made by pouring the oil and vinegar, separately, and to taste, over the greens. If you prefer the security of measuring and mixing your ingredients separately, we suggest the following simple, delicate dressing. To create an herb dressing, simply add 1 or 2 tablespoons fresh herbs of your choice to the following recipe. Let marinate at least 1 hour.

¼ cup fruity olive oil
1 tablespoon balsamic or other
    good quality red wine
    vinegar

Coarse salt to taste

Whisk the oil and vinegar together in small bowl. Sprinkle the salt directly over the salad greens. Pour just enough dressing over greens to moisten the salad. Toss salad just before serving. *Makes ¼ cup.*

GARLIC VINAIGRETTE

Delicious with tender green beans or other lightly cooked vegetables.

6 tablespoons fruity olive oil
3 garlic cloves, peeled and
    lightly crushed

2 tablespoons red wine vinegar
Coarse salt and freshly ground
    pepper to taste

Combine the olive oil, garlic, and red wine vinegar in a small bowl. Add the salt and pepper. Cover and let marinate for 2 hours or longer. Remove garlic cloves before using. Whisk lightly. *Makes ½ cup.*

ROSEMARY VINAIGRETTE

An aromatic dressing delicious with Grilled Butterflied Leg of Lamb (see page 222), duck salads, and potato salads.

¾ cup olive oil
¼ cup balsamic vinegar, or red wine
1 garlic clove, peeled and crushed

1 tablespoon minced fresh rosemary leaves, or 2 teaspoons dried rosemary leaves, crumbled
Coarse salt and freshly ground pepper to taste

If using dried rosemary, make the dressing at least a day ahead. Whisk together the oil, vinegar or wine, garlic, rosemary, salt, and pepper in a small bowl. Cover and let stand at least 3 hours. Remove the garlic clove and strain out the dried rosemary. *Makes 1 cup.*

ANCHOVY DRESSING

Good on Simple Artichokes (see page 135), green leaf salads with watercress, grilled fish, or any boiled beef.

½–1 can flat anchovy fillets, drained and finely chopped
¾ cup fruity olive oil
Juice of 1 lemon, or ¼ cup red wine vinegar

2 tablespoons minced fresh parsley
¼ teaspoon Dijon mustard (optional)
Freshly ground pepper to taste

Combine the anchovies in a small bowl with the olive oil, lemon juice or vinegar, parsley, mustard if using, and pepper. Whisk together. *Makes 1½ cups.*

ORANGE DRESSING WITH BASIL

Use on salads, spoon onto steamed mussels, or use as a marinade for broiled fish. This dressing has a sweet, refreshing taste. Increase the lemon juice for added tartness.

½ cup olive oil
4 tablespoons orange juice
2 tablespoons lemon juice
Zest of ½ orange

1 large garlic clove, peeled and lightly crushed
¼ cup fresh basil leaves, cut into thin slices
Coarse salt to taste

Combine the ingredients in a jar with a tight-fitting lid and shake. Strain out basil if desired. Let stand overnight. *Makes ¾ cup.*

LEMON MAYONNAISE

This is foolproof to make and a far cry from the mayonnaise in a jar, a product that has created a large contingent of mayonnaise haters. This lasts for up to 1 week refrigerated. Use with Salmon Scallops with Caviar (see page 183), to bind Insalata Russa (see page 66), or with freshly cooked lobster or other seafood.

1 egg, at room temperature
¼ teaspoon coarse salt

¾ cup olive oil
Juice of ½ lemon

Combine the egg, salt, and 3 tablespoons of the olive oil in a blender. Blend until the mixture is light in color. With blender on, pour in the remaining olive oil in a slow, steady stream. Stop pouring only if the oil is not being absorbed. If this occurs, blend without adding any more oil until the oil is absorbed, and then continue adding the remaining oil. Add the lemon juice and blend briefly. Adjust the seasonings. Scrape into a bowl. Cover tightly with plastic wrap and refrigerate up to 1 week. *Makes 1 cup.*

BASIL MAYONNAISE

Serve this lovely, light mayonnaise with Simple Artichokes (see page 135), poached fish, or as a spread in sandwiches.

2 egg yolks, at room
    temperature
½ teaspoon dry mustard
1 teaspoon red wine vinegar
1 garlic clove, peeled

1½ cups olive oil
1 cup firmly packed fresh basil
    leaves
Coarse salt and freshly ground
    pepper to taste

Place the egg yolks, mustard, vinegar, and garlic in a blender or food processor. With the motor on, add half the oil a bit at a time. Continue adding the oil in a slow, steady stream until thickened. Stop adding more oil only if it is not being absorbed. When this occurs, blend without adding any more oil until the oil is absorbed, and then continue adding the remaining oil. Scrape the mayonnaise into a bowl. Place the basil leaves in a blender or food processor with a couple of tablespoons of olive oil. Blend well. Whisk into the mayonnaise. Add salt, pepper, and more vinegar to taste. Cover tightly with plastic wrap and refrigerate for up to 1 week. *Makes 2 cups.*

A Ï O L I

This full-flavored mayonnaise elevates the humblest of meats, fish, and vegetables to sublime heights. Use with assorted cold meats such as lamb, pork, and beef, thinly sliced, or with seafood such as salmon or shrimp. Toss with garbanzo beans. Or arrange cooked vegetables such as beets, turnips, and green beans on a plate and serve with a dollop of aïoli on the side. We could go on and on. We use aïoli in Insalata Spagnola (page 69).

4 garlic cloves, peeled
Coarse salt

2 egg yolks, at room
temperature
¾ cup olive oil

Mash the garlic cloves with a little coarse salt using a mortar and pestle or the side of the blade of a chef's knife until a smooth paste forms. Place the egg yolks in a blender with a little salt. Blend until the egg is foamy. Add the olive oil gradually in a thin stream until the mixture thickens. Stop adding oil only if it is not being absorbed. When this occurs, blend without adding more oil until the oil is absorbed, and then continue adding the remaining oil. Add the garlic paste and blend for 1 or 2 seconds longer. Taste for salt. Scrape into a bowl. Cover tightly with plastic wrap and refrigerate for 2 or 3 days. *Makes 1 cup.*

MIMOSA SAUCE
hard-cooked egg yolk sauce

This golden-colored sauce is wonderful with thick asparagus stalks.

4 hard-cooked egg yolks
6 tablespoons olive oil
1 tablespoon Dijon or other
   good quality mustard

1 tablespoon white wine vinegar
2 tablespoons boiling water
Dash Worcestershire sauce
Coarse salt to taste

Combine the ingredients in a blender. Blend until smooth. Scrape into a bowl. Cover tightly with plastic wrap and refrigerate for up to several days. *Makes ¾ cup.*

FENNEL-FLAVORED MUSTARD SAUCE

Delicious with Gravlax All'Italiana (see page 178) and simple grilled fish.

1 teaspoon fennel seeds
¼ cup Dijon mustard
1 teaspoon dry mustard
2 tablespoons sugar

2 tablespoons white wine
   vinegar
⅓ cup fruity olive oil

Grind the fennel seeds to a powder using a mortar and pestle or an electric coffee grinder. Combine the ground fennel, mustards, sugar, and vinegar in a small bowl. Slowly add the olive oil, beating with a fork until creamy and thick. *Makes ¾ cup.*

CAPER SAUCE

Use with the Polpettone alla Campagnola (see page 217) or with other meats such as thinly sliced roast turkey.

2 tablespoons capers
4 canned flat anchovy fillets,
finely minced
4 large fresh sage leaves,
finely chopped, or 4 dried
sage leaves, crumbled

¾ cup fruity olive oil
Coarse salt and freshly ground
pepper to taste

Combine all the ingredients in a small bowl. Stir to mix well. *Makes about ¾ cup.*

SALSA VERDE

This brilliantly colored green sauce keeps its color and flavor for several days. The amounts given are a guide, so feel free to adapt this sauce. For example, substitute vinegar for lemon juice when used to accompany meats. Minced onion or shallots can also be added. This piquant sauce can be eaten as an appetizer spooned in hollowed-out cherry tomatoes, or by dipping crusty bread into a bowl of it. It is delicious with poached fish or roasted meats. Try to use parsley that has flat, bright green leaves as opposed to the very dark curly variety. Flat-leaf parsley is not necessary, but is always preferable in any recipe that calls for parsley. Taste a little of the parsley raw. If its flavor is too sharp, the sauce will be too strong.

1 cup flat-leaf parsley, minced

2 garlic cloves, peeled and
    minced

2 tablespoons capers, coarsely
    chopped

2–4 canned flat anchovy
    fillets, minced

¼ cup lemon juice

¾ cup fruity olive oil

In a small bowl, mix together the parsley, garlic, capers, and enough minced anchovy to give the sauce a salted punch. Stir in the lemon juice and olive oil. Mix thoroughly. Cover tightly with plastic wrap and refrigerate for up to 1 week. *Makes 1½ cups.*

SPICY SARDINIAN PARSLEY SAUCE

Excellent on grilled meats, fish, or chicken. Delicious poured over hot pasta, hard-cooked eggs, or as a marinade for oil-cured black olives.

1 cup loosely packed fresh
    parsley leaves, preferably
    flat-leaf parsley

2 garlic cloves, peeled

1 small fresh chile pepper,
    roasted, peeled, and
    seeded

Coarse salt

½ cup fruity olive oil

Make a paste using the parsley, garlic, chile pepper, and a generous amount of coarse salt in a mortar and pestle. Or, finely chop the ingredients with a chef's knife, mashing with the side of the blade. Place the chopped ingredients in a small bowl. Whisk in the olive oil. Season with additional salt, if necessary. *Makes about ¾ cup.*

SALSA CRUDA
raw   tomato   and   basil   sauce

A delicious sauce good on almost anything! Serve with grilled fish as in Grilled Swordfish with Salsa Cruda (see page 186). You can add finely diced red onion or finely minced fresh red chile pepper or cayenne, if desired.

**2 pounds firm ripe red
    tomatoes
2 garlic cloves, peeled and
    minced
¼ cup finely chopped fresh
    basil leaves**

**½ cup fruity olive oil
Coarse salt and freshly ground
    pepper to taste**

If the skin of the tomatoes is particularly tough, plunge them into boiling water for 5 seconds. Peel. Core, seed, and dice the tomatoes. Combine with the garlic, basil, and olive oil in a bowl. Season with salt and pepper. Marinate for 1 hour before using. *Makes 3 cups.*

TOMATO-BASIL SAUCE

An excellent basic sauce. Use with Timballo di Melanzane (see page 128) or for moistening pasta salads. Contrary to popular belief, cooking tomato sauces for hours succeeds only in making the tomatoes cloyingly sweet or slightly bitter.

1 can (28 ounces) good quality
  Italian-style peeled
  tomatoes
1–2 garlic cloves, peeled and
  minced
3–4 tablespoons olive oil

¼ cup finely chopped fresh
  parsley
2 tablespoons finely chopped
  fresh basil leaves, or 2
  teaspoons dried basil
  leaves, crumbled

Purée the tomatoes with their juice in a blender or food processor. Sauté the garlic briefly in the oil in a skillet. Add the tomatoes, parsley, and basil. Cook over moderately high heat until the sauce thickens and is reduced by one-third. The sauce will keep in the refrigerator from 1 to 2 days and in the freezer a month or so. *Makes 3 cups.*

TOMATO AND WATERCRESS SALSA

Serve as a bright, refreshing accompaniment to meats such as roast veal, lamb, or chicken. A generous spoonful on a plate adds a colorful note. Watercress has an unusual peppery flavor and is widely available. If you are able to find arugola, try it in place of the watercress, adding a squeeze of lemon juice. Arugola has a pronounced pungent, oaky flavor, and enjoys a devoted following.

1 large bunch watercress,
  leaves and tender stems
  only

4 large tomatoes
2–3 tablespoons fruity olive
  oil
Coarse salt to taste

Wash the watercress well. Dry the leaves and stems on paper towels. Roast, peel, and seed the tomatoes (see page 32). Chop into a small dice. Chop the watercress. Combine the watercress, tomatoes, olive oil, and salt in a medium bowl. *Serves 4 as a relish.*

SPICY ROASTED TOMATO, RED PEPPER, AND GARLIC SAUCE

Inspired by Elizabeth David, this vivid sauce is good with grilled fish or roasted chicken.

12 large garlic cloves
1 large tomato
1 large bottled roasted red
*   pepper, or 1 fresh red bell*
*   pepper*
1 very small fresh red or green
*   chile pepper, or cayenne*
*   to taste*

2 tablespoons fruity olive oil
1 teaspoon red wine vinegar or
*   to taste*
Coarse salt and freshly ground
*   pepper to taste*

Remove the loose papery skin from the garlic cloves, but do not peel. Bake the garlic cloves in a pan in a preheated 375° oven for 20 minutes. Roast the tomato over a gas flame, turning until lightly charred here and there. Core, peel, seed, and chop the tomato. If using a fresh red pepper, roast, peel, core, seed, and coarsely chop.

Roast the fresh chile pepper. Peel, seed, and mince. Place the tomato, red pepper, and chile pepper or cayenne in a large mortar or the bowl of a food processor fitted with a metal blade. Push the garlic out of their skins. Add the garlic to the tomato mixture and pound all the ingredients together with a pestle or process pulsing on and off until a smooth purée forms. Gradually add the olive oil. Season with vinegar, salt, and pepper. *Makes 1 cup.*

WINTER PESTO

Those of us who live in large urban areas are fortunate to find fresh basil nearly year round. There are times, however, when the summer-fresh taste of pesto calls and the fresh herb is unavailable or too expensive to use in great amounts. It is for just such times that we developed this Winter Pesto. The taste is similar to fresh basil pesto and the distinctive flavor of parsley is refreshing. Pesto stores well in either the freezer or refrigerator. We suggest freezing the sauce without the cheese. Just bring it back to room temperature and stir in the cheese before using. Without the cheese, the sauce is a welcome flavoring for soups or other sauces.

*2 large bunches fresh parsley,
stems removed and leaves
minced (2 cups)*
*3–4 tablespoons dried basil
leaves, crumbled*
3 garlic cloves, peeled
¼ cup walnut pieces

2 black peppercorns
1 cup olive oil
¼ cup grated Romano cheese
*½ cup grated Parmesan
cheese*
¼ teaspoon coarse salt

Combine the parsley in a food processor or blender with the basil, garlic, walnut pieces, peppercorns, and ¼ cup of the olive oil. Process until the mixture begins to form a thick paste. Add the cheeses and salt. With the processor running, slowly add the rest of the olive oil. To store, place in a plastic container and pour just enough olive oil over the pesto to cover so as to prevent sauce from darkening. *Makes 1½ cups.*

WINTER PESTO TWO

A strong, lusty "pesto" for the winter months. Great on pasta, also good as a filling for the tortas (see page 101).

*¾ cup Sun-dried Tomatoes
    (see page 276)*
¾ cup black olives in brine
*1 cup tightly packed fresh
    basil leaves, or ¼ cup
    dried basil leaves,
    crumbled*
¼ cup pine nuts

¼ cup walnuts
¼ cup grated Romano cheese
*¼ cup grated Parmesan
    cheese*
*Coarse salt and freshly ground
    pepper to taste*
½ cup olive oil

Place all the ingredients in a blender or the bowl of a food processor fitted with a metal blade. Process until the ingredients are well mixed but still have some texture. *Makes 1½ cups.*

SUN-DRIED TOMATOES

Always make plenty as they last a long time. They can be used in many ways—for example, in assorted antipasti, with cheeses, and in salads. The tomato-flavored oil can be used in Capellini with Sun-Dried Tomato "Pesto" (see page 78). It's the perfect way to preserve a bumper crop of garden fresh tomatoes.

Small tomatoes or cherry
*   tomatoes*
Coarse salt
Vinegar

Olive oil
Fresh rosemary, basil, or
*   thyme leaves (optional)*

Cut the small tomatoes into quarters or cherry tomatoes in half. Arrange the tomato pieces, cut-side up, on a baking sheet. Salt them. Place the baking sheet in a preheated 200° oven for about 7 hours. Watch tomatoes carefully to make sure they do not burn. When done, they should have a dried, shriveled appearance. As individual pieces dry completely, remove them, dip each in vinegar, and layer in a sterile glass jar. Cover the tomatoes completely with olive oil. Add the optional herbs. These tomatoes will last for months in or out of the refrigerator.

PESTO DI OLIVE

Pesto di olive is potent. Spread a very thin coating on crostini (see page 9), and it's also delicious on tomato halves. The spread lasts 1 week refrigerated.

½ cup oil-cured black olives,
   pitted
4 canned flat anchovy fillets
1 tablespoon minced fresh
   basil leaves, or 1
   tablespoon minced fresh
   rosemary leaves, or 1
   teaspoon dried rosemary
   leaves, crumbled

1 garlic clove, peeled
1 tablespoon capers
1 heaping tablespoon minced
   fresh fennel bulb
1 teaspoon grated orange zest
4 tablespoons olive oil
3–4 tablespoons lemon juice
Dash cayenne pepper

Combine all the ingredients in a food processor or blender. Process just until the ingredients are combined but before the mixture becomes too smooth. A little texture adds interest. For a coarser texture, finely chop the olives, anchovy fillets, garlic, and capers, and stir in remaining ingredients. *Makes ¾ cup.*

PINE NUT SAUCE

Use good, flavorful bread. Serve with crisp vegetables, such as celery stalks or wedges of fennel bulb, or with poached fish.

Generous handful dried bread
   without crusts (about 1
   ounce)
1 small garlic clove, peeled

Coarse salt
½ cup fresh pine nuts
1–2 tablespoons lemon juice
Freshly ground pepper

Soften the bread in water in a small bowl for several minutes. Drain. Squeeze the bread dry. Pound the garlic with coarse salt to a paste in a mortar and pestle. Or, finely chop with a chef's knife, mashing with the side of the blade. Add the pine nuts and crush to a paste. Add bread and incorporate. Season with lemon juice, salt, and pepper. If using a processor, combine the garlic paste, pine nuts, bread, lemon juice, salt, and pepper in the work bowl. Process until almost smooth. *Makes ⅔ cup.*

SPICY GREEN OLIVES WITH ROSEMARY

These olives are the perfect accompaniment to Homemade Ricotta (see page 92). They are also great served before dinner with wine. In Italy olives are prepared in an endless variety of ways. In the outdoor market in Catania we saw a staggering assortment of olives for sale. And in Palermo we remember seeing an olive vendor who had decorated his stand with garlands of fresh rosemary that perfumed the air. Use a good quality, unpitted olive. If sold in bulk, ask to taste one first. Look for crisp, firm olives.

Olive oil, enough to cover olives
5 sprigs (1 inch) fresh rosemary, or 2 tablespoons dried rosemary leaves
1–3 dried whole red chile peppers

4 garlic cloves, peeled and lightly crushed
10 peppercorns
3 long strips lemon peel
2 cups good-quality unpitted green olives in brine, drained

Heat ¼ cup of the olive oil gently in a saucepan over low heat with the rosemary, chile peppers, garlic, peppercorns, and lemon peel. When seasonings release their fragrance, pour the mixture over the olives. Add more olive oil to cover. Cover tightly with plastic wrap and marinate. These olives last indefinitely. *Makes 2 cups.*

SICILIAN GREEN OLIVE SALAD

The briny flavor of the olives is set off by the fresh herbal flavor of celery and the biting, sweet taste of the onion. Accompany with crusty bread.

2 cups cracked large green olives in brine, drained if necessary
½ medium red onion, peeled
2 large celery stalks with leaves, strings removed

Olive oil
Red wine vinegar
Coarse salt to taste

Remove the olives from the brine and rinse in cold water. Drain thoroughly. Cut the red onion into ¼-inch-thick slices. Cut the celery into ½-inch-thick pieces and coarsely chop the celery leaves. Combine all the ingredients in a bowl and toss with enough olive oil to lightly coat. Add the vinegar and salt to taste. Cover and allow to marinate several hours or overnight. *Serves 6 to 8 as an appetizer.*

SWEET CHERRIES IN VINEGAR

Cherries in vinegar is a beautiful holiday dish to serve with traditional turkey or a roasted loin of pork. The cherries can be prepared for canning, if desired. Layer the ingredients in a mason jar and proceed as you would normally for preserving. This is an ideal dish for using White Wine Vinegar Flavored with Black Peppercorns (see page 19). The bite of the pepper combined with the sweetness of the cherries and the freshness of the vinegar is bracing and unusual.

2 pounds sweet bing or Queen Anne cherries, pitted
¾ cup sugar
1 teaspoon whole cloves
2 sticks cinnamon, broken into pieces

3–4 cups good-quality white wine vinegar
Peel of 1 lemon

In a glass bowl suitable for presentation, layer the cherries with the sugar, cloves, and cinnamon pieces. Continue until you have used all of the cherries. Boil the white wine vinegar with the lemon peel in a saucepan. Pour over the layered cherries while still hot. Refrigerate. Serve cold. *Makes 4 cups.*

CRANBERRY-MINT RELISH

This brilliantly colored sauce is the ideal accompaniment to a fresh or smoked holiday turkey or roast loin of pork. We love the sweet, tart flavor and the deep red color it lends to a plate of Chicken Breasts Poached in Orange Juice and Sage (see page 231). When fresh cranberries are plentiful during fall and winter, buy several extra bags and store in the freezer.

1 pound fresh or fresh frozen cranberries

½ cup fresh mint leaves, finely chopped, or 2 tablespoons dried mint leaves, crumbled

1 cup sugar

Juice of 1 orange

1 cup water

Chop the cranberries roughly with a knife or in a food processor. Place all the ingredients in a heavy enamel or stainless steel saucepan and bring to a boil, stirring occasionally. Lower the heat and simmer the sauce until the sugar is melted and the mixture begins to thicken, about 10 minutes. Refrigerate before serving. *Makes 3 cups.*

BIBLIOGRAPHY

Artusi, Pellegrino, *La Scienza in Cucina e L'Arte di Mangiar Bene.* Firenze: Marzacco, 1959.

Beard, James, *Menus for Entertaining.* New York: Delacorte, 1965.

————, *American Cooking.* Boston: Little, Brown, 1972.

Benini, Zenone, *La Cucina di Casa Mia.* Italy: Olimpia, 1975.

Boni, Ada, *Italian Regional Cooking.* New York: Bonanza Books, 1969.

————, *Il Talismano della Felicita.* Italy: Casa Editrice Colombo, 1983.

Brillat-Savarin, Jean-Anthelme, *The Physiology of Taste.* Translated by M. F. K. Fisher. New York: Knopf, 1971.

Bugialli, Giuliano, *The Fine Art of Italian Cooking.* New York: Times Books, 1977.

————, *Giuliano Bugialli's Classic Techniques of Italian Cooking.* New York: Simon & Schuster, 1982.

Child, Julia, Louisette Bertholle, and Simone Beck, *Mastering the Art of French Cooking,* Vol. One. New York: Knopf, 1975.

————, *Mastering the Art of French Cooking*, Vol. Two. New York: Knopf, 1970.

David, Elizabeth, *Classics: Mediterranean Food, French Country Cooking, Summer Cooking*. New York: Knopf, 1980.

————, *Italian Food*. London: Penguin, 1976.

Distefano, Bianca, *Cucina Che Vai, Natura Che Trovi*. Palermo: Edikronos, 1981.

Fisher, M. F. K., *The Art of Eating*. New York: Vintage Books, 1976.

————, *With Bold Knife and Fork*. New York: Putnam's, 1968.

The Gourmet Cookbook, Vol. One. New York: Gourmet Books, Inc., 1974.

The Gourmet Cookbook, Vol. Two. New York: Gourmet Books, Inc., 1974.

Harris, Lloyd J., *The Book of Garlic*. Berkeley: Aris Books, 1979.

Hazan, Marcella, *The Classic Italian Cookbook*. New York: Knopf, 1976.

————, *More Classic Italian Cooking*. New York: Knopf, 1978.

Johnston, Mireille, *Cuisine of the Sun*. New York: Random House, 1976.

Kamman, Madeleine M., *When French Women Cook: A Gastronomic Memoir*. New York: Atheneum, 1976.

Olney, Judith, *Summer Food*. New York: Atheneum, 1978.

Olney, Richard, *Simple French Food*. New York: Atheneum, 1974.

———— (ed.), *The Good Cook, Technique and Recipes*. Alexandria, Va.: Time-Life Books, 1979.

Romagnoli, Margaret, and Franco G. Romagnoli, *The Romagnolis' Meatless Cookbook*. Boston: Atlantic Monthly Press, 1976.

Rombauer, Irma S., and Marion Becker, *The Joy of Cooking*. Indianapolis: Bobbs-Merrill, 1983.

Root, Waverley, *The Best of Italian Cooking*. New York: Grosset & Dunlap, 1974.

————, *The Food of Italy*. New York: Random House, 1971.

————, *Herbs and Spices*. New York: McGraw-Hill, 1980.

————, *Food*. New York: Simon & Schuster, 1980.

Sala, Orietta, *Primi Piatti*. Italy: A. Vallardi, 1983.

Stelvio, Maria, *Cucina Triestina*. Trieste: Stabilimento Tipografico Nazionale, 1980.

Toklas, Alice B., *The Alice B. Toklas Cookbook*. Garden City, New York: Doubleday, 1960.

Waters, Alice L., *Chez Panisse Menu Cookbook*. New York: Random House, 1982.

INDEX

Aïoli, 267
Almonds, Peaches Stuffed with
  Amaretti, Chocolate,
  and, 247–48
Amaretti
  Peaches Stuffed with
    Almonds, Chocolate,
    and, 247–48
  Peaches with Marsala,
    Whipped Cream, and,
    246–47
Anchovy(-ies), 7
  Dressing, 264–65
  Red Bell Peppers Stuffed
    with Tomato and, 163
  Spinach with, 153–54
Andrews, Colman, 252
Anisette, Cantaloupe with, 240
Antipasto, Sun-Dried Tomatoes
  and Mozzarella, 65–66
Apples Stuffed with Pine Nuts,
  241
Arista, 220–21
Artichokes
  Bread-Stuffed, 137

Artichokes *(cont'd)*
  Roman-Style, 138–39
  Simple, 135–36
  in Tomato Sauce, 139–40
Artusi, Pellegrino, 230
Arugola, 46, 47
  Carpaccio with Parmesan
    and, 209
  in *Insalata Mista Elevata*, 47
Asparagus, 141
  to cook, 142
  Julienne, Carrot and, 61
  Simple, 141–42
  with Tomatoes and Pine
    Nuts, 142–43
Avocado
  and Ricotta Salata, in Chile
    Pepper Oil, 96
  Salad of Tomato, Red Onion
    and, 55

Balsamic Vinegar
  Chicken in, 232–34
  Roasted Red or Yellow
    Onions in, 160–61

Basil
  Hard-Cooked Eggs and
    Whole Leaves of,
    102–3
  Mayonnaise, 266–67
  and Mint Vinaigrette, Salad
    of Squid in, 200–1
  Olive Oil Flavored with,
    Whole Roasted
    Tomatoes with, 173
  Orange Dressing with, 265
  Penne with Tomato,
    Mozzarella, and, 73–74
  Pesto. *See* Pesto
  and Ricotta Tart, 124
  Roasted Red Pepper Salad
    with, 56
  Salmon Marinated with, Raw,
    177–78
  Tomato and Mozzarella
    Slices with, 63–64
  and Tomato Sauce, 271–72
    Raw, 271
    Spicy, Mussels with, 196–
    97
  and Zucchini Frittata, 105–6